O.J. SIMPSON
AMERICAN HERO—AMERICAN TRAGEDY

In the pre-dawn hours of June 13, 1994, the bodies of O.J. Simpson's beautiful ex-wife Nicole and a male companion were found lying in a pool of blood outside her elegant Brentwood townhouse.

In the days that followed, more details emerged:

- The stormy love-hate relationship between O.J. and Nicole was powered by violent fights triggered by the football hero's explosive fits of jealousy.
- The New Year's Eve episode that ended with a battered Nicole in the hospital and O.J. in court.
- O.J.'s open letter, which many interpreted as a suicide note, in which he insisted "I have nothing to do with Nicole's murder. I loved her. I always have and always will."
- Rumors of evidence that includes a bloody glove found at O.J.'s $5 million mansion, bloodstains in his driveway and in his white Ford Bronco, and cuts and scratches on his body.

Today, O.J. Simpson stands accused of murder!

O.J. SIMPSON
AMERICAN HERO
AMERICAN TRAGEDY

Marc Cerasini

PINNACLE BOOKS
WINDSOR PUBLISHING CORP.

PINNACLE BOOKS are published by

Windsor Publishing Corp.
850 Third Avenue
New York, NY 10022

Copyright © 1994 by Marc Cerasini

The P logo Reg U.S. Pat & TM Off. Pinnacle is a trademark of Windsor Publishing Corp.

First Printing: June, 1994

Printed in the United States of America

Credits for Cover Photos:

Stephen Harvey/Shooting Star,
Harry Langdon/Shooting Star,
R. Davis/Shooting Star.

ACKNOWLEDGEMENTS

To my editor Sarah Gallick, who asked me to do it . . . But most of all for Alice Alfonsi. People often say that without her it couldn't have been done. I mean it—it couldn't have been done without you.

If we can survive this, we can survive anything.

"Show me a hero and I will write you a tragedy."

— F. Scott Fitzgerald

"If there's any truth in Robert Browning's
philosophy, 'A minute's success pays [for] the
failure of years,' then a host of . . . celebrities
should realize that the opposite is equally
true: a minute's failure can erase the success
of years."

— Norman O. Unger, *Jet* magazine,
February 18, 1985

When you shall these unlucky deeds relate,
Speak of me as I am. Nothing extenuate,
Nor set down aught in malice. Then must you
speak
Of one that loved not wisely, but too well . . .

— William Shakespeare, *Othello*, V.II

One

The first sign of trouble seemed to arrive some time between 10:30 and 11:00 P.M. on a balmy Sunday night in Southern California.

Neighbors heard the frenzied sound of barking dogs coming from behind the shaded walls of the condominiums and town houses scattered along Bundy Drive. Such a sound would be a mundane one in many American neighborhoods, but not in the pricey, upscale suburb of quiet Brentwood, a town situated in the poshest section of Los Angeles, just a stone's throw from Rodeo Drive and Beverly Hills.

Things are usually pretty quiet on Bundy Drive—the wealthy residents pay a lot of money to make sure it stays that way, and they can certainly afford it. But tonight things would be different.

The dogs barked for almost fifteen minutes, says one resident of a nearby condominium complex who wished to remain anonymous. "That was unusual" she told reporters from ABC News, "this is usually a pretty quiet neighborhood."

In time, and with the realization of the horror that occurred just outside of their gardens, gates and doors, other neighbors would swear that they heard the sound of gunshots and even screams, but these statements would soon be discounted by the authorities. They were, the police said, the result of fear, of hysteria, of grief, and of shock.

As far as the authorities are concerned, the only sound that disturbed the residents of Bundy Drive on the night of June 12, 1994, was the barking of a single dog, until another animal who lived nearby chimed in, as dogs will. No one investigated the noise, and soon the sound of barking dwindled, and died away. Peace was restored to this affluent, closely-knit community—but it would not remain peaceful for long.

Los Angeles is a place where, in the words of the rabidly East Coast filmmaker Woody Allen, "feet never touch pavement." Brentwood, a part of West Hollywood, is the kind of community where residents would rather travel a block to the grocery store in their BMWs, Porsches and Jaguars, than actually take a walk.

No one, they say, gets mugged in Brentwood, because there is no one on the sidewalks to get mugged. So it is really no surprise that the two bodies, a young, well-dressed man and a beautiful blonde woman, who lay sprawled on the tile sidewalk near the gate outside of the taupe-colored, Spanish-style split level town house in pools of their own blood weren't discovered until ten minutes after midnight, by a neighbor who immediately called 911.

Within minutes after the grisly discovery, uniformed and plain clothes policemen swarmed the area in front and in back of the $700,000 town house, a property shaded by graceful palm trees and decorated with brilliantly-colored exotic flowers and sprawling, meticulously-manicured lawns.

The area immediately surrounding the town house was quickly cordoned off. The police used the bright yellow crime scene tape—a sight familiar to urban residents, yet far from common to the comfortable residents of Brentwood.

By one A.M. the ribbons closed off the sidewalk, preventing the curious gathering crowd from seeing the blood and the bodies.

Yellow ribbons also encircled the Jeep Grand Cherokee and the white Ferrari convertible—its top still down—that were parked side by side in the back of the sprawling town house.

In short order, the police tentatively established that one of the murder victims—the woman—was a resident of the posh Bundy Drive split-level. Her body was mutilated—her throat was slashed, her body bruised, and her neck and breasts stabbed over a dozen times.

Within nine hours after the chilling discovery, the female victim was positively identified as Nicole Brown Simpson, the thirty-five-year-old ex-wife of football superstar O.J. Simpson.

Ironically it was her ex-husband, the very man who would be arrested days later for the two murders, who made the positive identification for the Los Angeles County Coroner's Office.

The other murder victim, described as a twenty-five-year old male, whose blood-spattered corpse was discovered next to Nicole Simpson's, was not positively identified until the next day. His name was Ronald Lyle Goldman. He was a part-time male model and full-time waiter at one of the many popular restaurants that catered to the toney tastes of the residents of Brentwood. The restaurant where he worked, called Mezzaluna, was located on San Vincente Boulevard, only a short trip down Montana Avenue and around the corner from Bundy Drive and Nicole Simpson's townhouse. The restaurant had hosted a dinner party earlier that very evening, when Nicole and nine companions had dined and celebrated—O.J. Simpson was not among the group.

At the time, Goldman was on duty, but he was not the Simpson party's waiter. Acquaintances say Goldman had known Nicole Simpson for a few months, and was even seen driving Nicole's white Ferrari convertible around Brentwood—sometimes in the company of the statuesque blond, sometimes alone. Some acquaintances said that Nicole had taken an interest in Goldman's modeling/acting career, and was trying to help him get his first big break. Others maintained that he was just another member of the toney set, a fortunate beneficiary of the wealthy Nicole's interest and attention.

Goldman's past, as well as his relationship with Nicole Simpson, would be the subject of much speculation in the coming days. Among those who knew them from the restaurant, or the upscale health club called The Gym, where they both worked out, few thought that his relationship with the ex-Mrs. Simpson was merely a platonic one.

Whatever their relationship, however, it was just one piece of a complex puzzle that would lead inevitably to a double murder.

Shockingly, when the police finally crossed the blood-splattered sidewalk and entered Nicole Simpson's town house, they found two children from her marriage to the football superstar.

Five-year-old Justin Ryan Simpson, and his seven-year-old sister, Sydney Brook Simpson, were in bed. They had slept through the carnage. No doubt Sydney was especially tired. She'd had a busy day, as both her mother and her celebrity father had attended a dance recital in which she had performed to wild applause. The dinner party at Mezzaluna had actually been held in her honor, and it had been a long day for such a little girl.

Authorities carefully removed the two children from the crime scene at about the same time as police forensic experts arrived. Lugging cases of equipment, the forensic team began their grisly task. They found the two bodies, sprawled at the bottom of the steps leading to the front door of the town house, right near the gate. The victims were surrounded by a "sea of blood" and some members of the uniformed police had the unenviable task of "tidying up" the scene so that the technicians could get closer to the bodies. They used white towels to soak up the blood, while other investigators photographed the crime scene and searched for a murder weapon.

One neighbor, who saw the bodies, said that Nicole's appeared as if she had been struggling with her assailant, and her companion was also quite bloodied.

The search for Nicole's ex-husband, O.J. Simpson, was officially launched by about one-thirty A.M., Monday morning. Unknown to the police at that time, the object of their manhunt was on a red-eye flight out of Los Angeles.

At that point in their investigation, the Los Angeles authorities maintained, O. J. Simpson was not considered a suspect.

"He is being interviewed as a possible witness," stated LAPD Officer Sandra Castello the next day, "[he is] not necessarily an eyewitness, but he is considered a witness at this time."

By Monday afternoon, June 13th, things

suddenly took a very different turn. The approximate time of the victim's deaths was established by the coroner's office. The police determined that the sports legend, a winner of the Heisman Trophy, a member of the Football Hall of Fame, and a motion picture and television star, had boarded American Airlines flight 668 for Chicago at 11:45 P.M.—not much more, and perhaps less than one hour after the slayings.

"In crimes of this nature, always look for the most likely suspect—in this case, it was the victim's ex-husband, who had both the motive and the ability to commit the crimes . . . the fact that he had boarded a flight out of Los Angeles within an hour after the slayings did not look good," said one anonymous informer within the Los Angeles police department, in one of the many questionable leaks that were to surface during the next few days.

Officially, LAPD Commander David Gascon was more guarded when he went on record, stating simply that "we are not going to rule anyone out."

The Los Angeles police wanted answers to a number of vital questions. Why was O. J.

Simpson on a flight to Chicago? Where was he at the time of his ex-wife's murder? Did Simpson run from police? Should he now be considered a fugitive?

It was later established that the sports legend was on his way to Chicago for a scheduled promotional trip, a trip that had been planned weeks in advance. According to published reports, Simpson had actually made hotel reservations at the O'Hare Plaza-Hotel six days prior to his arrival—but the police could not know this at the time, and Simpson's trip looked very suspicious in the eyes of the authorities in Los Angeles.

When O. J. Simpson was notified in Chicago, at about 7:30 A.M., Central Daylight Time, of his ex-wife's murder, he hurriedly checked out of the O'Hare Plaza Hotel and headed back to Los Angeles. According to his lawyer, he was so upset by the news that he crushed a glass in his hand, and cut himself. That would explain the bloody towels found in his room at the O'Hare Plaza-Hotel by Chicago police, who investigated the room at the request of Los Angeles authorities.

A distraught O.J. Simpson took American Airlines flight 1691 out of Chicago and arrived at LAX at 11:08 A.M., Pacific Daylight Time. He immediately headed for his Brentwood home, where he arrived at 11:30. Once there, he contacted his lawyer, Howard Weitzman, and was met by uniformed police, who took him to headquarters for questioning.

The interrogation by Los Angeles homicide detectives lasted over four hours, and at one point O.J. Simpson was photographed by a television crew wearing plastic handcuffs, with his hands strapped behind his back. Los Angeles television station KCOE broadcasted this image on its nightly news, and soon this disturbing picture was broadcast nationwide.

The sight of this football legend, this Heisman Trophy-winner, this proud member of the Football Hall of Fame, this television and motion picture star, this sports broadcaster, this millionaire, this African-American icon wearing handcuffs shocked the nation.

Stunned, America asked itself how? How could the horrible events of the last twelve hours have happened? How could things have led to this? How could one of America's best-loved athletes be a murderer? What could drive this man, who had everything any man could ever want, to kill?

How did it happen—and why?

Two

Success seemed to come early to Orenthal James Simpson, so early that, upon reflection, it looks as if he was always destined for something very special. But that sense of destiny was far from the mind of a young, somewhat scrawny, pigeon-toed and bowlegged boy growing up in the lower-middle-class section of San Francisco's Potrero Hill—much less of a ghetto now, after years of gentrification, than it was back in the 1950s and '60s, when Orenthal was growing up.

Born on July 9, 1947, he was a welcome addition to an otherwise rocky household that already had two children—a boy, Leon and a girl, Carmelita. There never seemed to be enough money, and the family was always struggling financially.

Not long after Orenthal James was born, another girl, named Shirley—came along.

Economically, things got worse for the family, and when Orenthal was just four years old, his father left his wife and family.

With the departure of Jimmy Simpson, Eunice Durton Simpson was now responsible for raising all four children on her own meager salary earned as an orderly at San Francisco General Hospital—a place where she would continue to work for 32 years, eventually rising to become a psychiatric technician.

While his mother was cursed with financial woes, the very young Orenthal was afflicted, too—physically. He was suffering from a disease called rickets, a malady detected when he was just two-years-old.

Rickets is a disease of poverty. It is caused by a nutritional deficiency in childhood. A child's skeleton needs an adequate amount of calcium and phosphates. If it doesn't get them, the child's bones become deformed as they grow.

The most common cause of rickets is deficiency of vitamin D. Without vitamin D, the human body cannot properly absorb calcium from the intestines into the blood and eventually into the bones.

Vitamin D is found in fat containing animal substances such as oily fish, butter, egg yolk, liver, and fish liver oils. There are also small amounts in human and animal milk. The vitamin is also made in the body through the action of sunlight on the skin.

Rickets occurs primarily in poor countries and in communities where babies receive inadequate vitamin D in the diet and simultaneously do not get enough sunlight.

Breast milk alone cannot provide all of a baby's needs for vitamin D. A breastfed baby who gets little sun is at risk of getting rickets unless it is given vitamin D supplements.

These days, in the U.S. and other developed countries, vitamin D supplements are now routinely given to infants. In addition, the vitamin is added to foods such as cows milk, margarine and breakfast cereals.

The most striking feature of advanced rickets is deformity of the legs and spine. Typically there is bowing of the legs and in infants, flattening of the head as a result of softness of the skull.

Infants with rickets often sleep poorly and show delay in crawling and walking. Other features include spinal curvature, enlargements of the wrists and ankles, pelvic pain, a tendency to fracture, and muscle weakness.

Rickets made a marked impact on the physique of young Orenthal Simpson. He was left with abnormally skinny legs. In addition he was made both bow-legged and pigeon toed, another side effect.

A child like Orenthal would be routinely

treated with vitamin D supplements. He would be given plenty of milk to provide calcium. The treatment generally continues until X-rays show healing.

[Note:There are undesireable side effects to excessive use of vitamin D supplements.]

A doctor who examined the boy's already deformed legs told Eunice Simpson that young Orenthal needed, at the very least, braces to correct them. Unfortunately, his financially-strapped mother could not afford braces or any other complex medical intervention, and so a compromise was reached.

Instead of braces, which Orenthal surely needed, or corrective surgery, which was also an option, he wore a pair of specially-designed orthopedic shoes connected by an iron bar—he wore these heavy, clumsy "implements of torture" as he called them, every single day from the time his disorder was discovered until he was five years old. But even this humiliating and limiting health problem did not crush this underprivledged child blessed with a fierce determination to succeed.

Perhaps it was these very setbacks that forged the young man's seemingly indomitable spirit, and his determination to physically dominate his environment—on the athletic field and later on, in his domestic life as well.

As O.J. himself put it, "every day until I was almost five, I'd be shufflin' around the house. But then my legs improved and I got to be a very rowdy character."

From his early years on, O.J. looked up to his hard-working mother. "You just don't know what it is to be 8 years old," said an adult O.J., "and have all your friends think that you have the best mother in the neighborhood."

Eunice was devoted to her children, and to O.J., she would always be the "most important person" in his life.

When Orenthal was about 9 years old, Eunice took the whole family on vacation to visit her sister in Las Vegas, Nevada. At the time she was working the grave yard shift—midnight to morning—at the hospital. This was her two weeks off—her only two week vacation. Yet when she saw her young son was sad about missing his first Little League game, she didn't hesitate to sacrifice even that to make him happy.

What Eunice did next became something indelibly imbedded in O.J.'s memories—it was the kind of selfless act that truly proves to a child that he or she is loved, and is special.

O.J. would tell the story of that vacation during his 1985 acceptance speech upon being inducted into the Pro Football Hall of Fame in Canton, Ohio.

"I [remembered] I had to play in a Little League—my first Little League baseball game and I was moping around. She noticed how sad I was and . . . she drove me 700 miles—in the middle of this vacation. She took me 700 miles back to San Francisco so I wouldn't miss my first Little League game . . ."

Fighting back tears, O.J. looked at his mother, "I love you for that," he said. Bursting with pride for her son, Eunice's own tears flowed as the audience broke out into prolonged applause.

O.J. would also thank his father, Jimmy Simpson, in that famous speech.

"Now what do you say about your dad, you know? There are people . . . they're raised in broken homes. Even though my dad didn't live under the same roof as us, during most of my youth, he was always there . . . I always had a father. I love you for it."

Though his presence was not a day-to-day one, Jimmy served as an off-premises disciplinarian to his son. When any serious discipline problems arose, Eunice would call Jimmy. After getting into trouble, the young Orenthal would often nervously anticipate facing his father—and his father's belt.

Yet, though he loved his father, and appreciated Jimmy's presence in his life, an adult O.J. would later express regrets over not having an intact family and day-to-day dad in his life.

"Except for holidays," he would say in a 1975 article for *Parents* magazine, "when I was growing up I rarely saw my father. I resented his absence, especially when I became a teenager, and was trying to find out who I was. I really needed a man around then for guidance.

"I get along with my father now, but it's taken years for me to come to terms with my feelings."

Ironically, in the course of O.J.'s own life, he would come to leave his own children without an intact family, as well. Just two years before the break-up of his first marriage, O.J. expressed fear in that same *Parents* magazine article that he would follow in his father's footsteps.

As Orenthal entered his teens, his life became rockier. He became a self-described "rowdy character," getting involved in some minor scrapes with the law. He was even arrested several times.

In 1976 Simpson told a *Playboy* magazine interviewer that he was arrested a couple of times, mostly for "fighting, and once for stealing, which I didn't do."

He elaborated by speaking candidly about what he says was his first and only arrest for theft.

"I don't want to make myself sound good," he said in the *Playboy* interview, but one time our club was giving a dance and instead of buying the wine, the guys decided to rip it off. I kept tellin' 'em we had the money to buy the stuff, but no, they wanted to steal it.

"I didn't even go into the liquor store with 'em. I waited outside and when they came out, we walked around the corner—and right into the hands of the police."

Later, in a 1987 interview with *Sports Illustrated*, O.J. recalls things a bit differently, admitting: "We were all underage, of course, and we didn't have any money, but we devised ways of getting liquor anyhow."

In this version of the story, four or five of his club would go into a liquor store and two would pretend to start a fight. While the store owner rushed to separate the combantants, the other kids would quickly stuff bottles under their jackets.

Being on the "refreshment committee," according to this later account, meant that a club member had to hit a few stores to get enough for the party.

No matter the exact circumstances, the outcome for Orenthal regarding that big, special dance was the same. He never got there.

"We'd planned that dance for months, had sent out hundreds of invitations, had done all *kinds* of advance work—we were calling it The Affair of the Year—and there we were, up against the wall, and then in jail."

WINKY, THE CLUBS, AND THE 'HOOD

Never a shy child, as he matured Orenthal became even more gregarious. At high school dances, the young man was often seen wearing a long white hat that slouched down over his eyes. When he sat down for his 1976 *Playboy* interview, he reminisced about those days.

"If I saw a girl who looked good, I'd go right up to her and start rappin', even if she was with a guy," he told *Playboy*. "I didn't care *what* the dude said, 'cause I'd tell him,

'Hey, I'm talkin' to her, not *you*, man. If she don't *want* me to talk to her, she'll *tell* me she don't want me to talk to her.'

"It rarely got into punches, because most of the dudes didn't want to fight me."

In fact, as *Playboy* reported in the interview, Orenthal—or Waterhead, a much less cherished nickname that he was tagged with back then—got quite a reputation as a tough guy, a reputation that, as an adult, O.J. is quick to deflate.

"You gotta realize that San Francisco isn't a big town and it ain't that hard to develop a reputation," O.J. told *Playboy*.

Most of O.J.'s "reputation" was gained from a single altercation he had with a punk called Winky, who belonged to the toughest club—which was much closer to what we would call today a gang—in San Francisco, a club called the Roman Gents. He recalled those days in detail in the *Playboy* interview.

Like the gangs of today, some of them wore special jackets, the 1950s and '60s version of gang "colors," O.J. explained. But the level of violence—and firearms—existing in gang culture today was not prevalent when O.J. was growing up, and some of his gang or as he sometimes called them, "club" experiences sound almost Damon Runyon-esque by today's brutal youth-gang standards.

One night there was a dance at the Booker T. Washington Community Center and, O.J. told his *Playboy* interviewer, an older dude came up to him and started hassling him. "What did you say about my sister?" he screamed, getting into Orenthal's face in an aggressive and threatening manner.

"I'd heard of Winky—just about everyone had—but I didn't know that was who this was so I just said, 'Hey man, I don't know your sister. I don't even know you,' " O.J. told *Playboy*.

"It wasn't cool to fight in the community center, so the guy started walking away, but he was still talkin' crap to me and I yelled back, 'Fuck you, too, man!' "

A few minutes later he saw the same guy with a bunch of Roman Gents, who were attempting to hold him back. The punk finally broke free of his club members and ran back up to Orenthal shouting "Motherfucker, I'm gonna kick your ass!" The music stopped and the room got quiet. All eyes in the crowded auditorium were on the two youths, and then O.J. heard the bad news—everybody was whispering "Winky's gettin' ready to fight."

Winky!

"Damn," O.J. told the *Playboy* interviewer. "I didn't want to fight *him.*"

The head of the community center came to O.J.'s rescue, and led him out of the auditorium. He couldn't leave though, because Winky and his friends were waiting outside for him.

As O.J. recalled the episode for his *Playboy* interview, he eventually eluded the Roman Gents, and sneaked home, but for the next couple of weeks people from Potrero Hill were constantly chasing him down and saying things like, "Hey man, Winky's boys are on their way over to get you," and he would have to make himself scarce. His social life was in a shambles, and he was afraid to even venture out and play ball.

Eventually, things got so hot that young Orenthal had to be sent to Las Vegas, to live with his uncle for the summer.

"When I went back, I was sure things had cooled off," he told *Playboy*, "but one night I'm comin' out of a party and who do I bump into? Right. Winky and his boys."

Orenthal was in for a surprise, however, because the reckless courage he had displayed at the Booker T. Washington auditorium before served him in good stead.

"Instead of fightin' with me, he says, 'Hey, little dude, you got a lot of guts, come on in and have a drink with us.' I was as leery as hell, but there wasn't much I could do . . . so I went inside and Winky told everybody, 'This is our little dude. From now on, anybody fucks with him gotta fuck with *us.*'

O.J. told *Playboy* that after that episode, throughout his high school years, most of the guys around San Francisco knew who he was."

All things considered, Orenthal wasn't a bad kid—just mischievous. Some of his ways had to do with the place where he grew up.

Make no mistake, Potrero Hill was a ghetto at that time, but this was the period before the scourge of gang violence and drugs were to destroy generations of urban black youths. This was also before the well-meaning but misguided "Great Society" programs of the 1960s really kicked in.

Social programs like public housing and welfare, as virtually everyone now realizes, were ultimately destructive and encouraged the break-up of the black family by replacing the authority figure of the father in the home with the paternal state. These programs often dismantled black neighborhoods

and communities replacing them instead
with cold and impersonal government-subsi-
dized housing projects.

According to O.J. Simpson, Potrero Hill
might have been a ghetto, but it was hearth
and home to him.

"Blacks talk about other blacks bein' your
brothers and sisters, and that applies even
more in the projects, where everybody's
momma is your momma and three or four
nights a week you'll be eatin' over at somebody else's house."

Make no mistake, even then, according to
California state statistics, almost seventy percent of the residents of Potrero Hill were on
welfare when O.J. was growing up, but the
work ethic and a strong sense of personal
dignity among black families was not yet
crushed by "benevolent" government programs. As Simpson himself puts it:

"It's bullshit to think [the people of
Potrero Hill] sat on their asses waiting for
Government checks, because fathers were al-
ways out there looking for jobs . . .

"To me, Potrero Hill was America the
Beautiful, and I think most of the people
who lived there felt the same way."

The sense of community, of shared con-
cern and shared interests, was strong.

"I remember that at world-series time, everybody would crowd around a radio to listen to the games, and when the national anthem was played, the whole room would stand up.

*"Every*body—mothers, fathers, kids—would be on their feet.

"Mostly, I remember all the adventures we had," O.J. recalled in a 1976 interview.

"There was a polliwog pond, railroad tracks, a lumberyard and lots of factories nearby, and in the summer, when there wasn't anything to do, somebody would say, 'Hey, let's go hit the pie factory.'

"So we'd go down there, sneaking around the fence and set up what looked like a little bucket brigade, and we'd steal maybe thirty pies. My favorite was blackberry: man that was *good.*"

He also recalls similar expeditions to the Hostess Bakery and the local milk factory.

"We had a good group of dudes and my best friends then are still my best friends now. We also had the toughest gang on Potrero Hill; couldn't nobody whip us on the Hill."

While it might have been dangerous to belong to a gang, it was not as dangerous then as it is today. As far as O.J. was concerned, "it was more dangerous *not* to [belong].

"There was never any blame attached to it, and if you weren't in one, you had to be kind of goofy or else just plain out of it."

When Orenthal was thirteen, he joined his first gang, called the Gladiators. "I was the president; and me and all my little cronies got these great burgundy-satin jackets that I later learned were baseball windbreakers.

"There were about fourteen of us, and we stayed on Potrero Hill and never dealt with any gang outside the district, because we were too young."

As he got older, the stakes went up a bit. "I joined my first *fighting* gang when I got to junior high and got with the Persian Warriors. There was about twenty-five guys in the club and I think I was the only one who didn't live in the Fillmore District."

As with most of the "real" gangs, there was a ladies' auxiliary—the Persian Parettes, "the best female club in San Francisco.

"I was fourteen when the Parettes came into my life and, man, they gave me an *education.*"

Of course, things were not all fun and games and an *"education"* for young Orenthal.

"We did a pretty good amount of fighting and the big showdowns would usually take

place on holidays, when everybody would get
on down to Market Street.

"You'd hear the cats sayin', 'You gonna be
at the Golden Gate Theatre tomorrow? The
Roman Gents are gonna fight the Sheiks!' I
joined a club called the Superiors when I
got to high school, and that's when we
started steppin' out of all that rowdy shit and
started giving dances instead."

It was a pretty profitable time for Orenthal. One year the Superiors rented a hall in
the Sheraton-Palace Hotel and gave a Halloween party. The turnout was phenomenal
and the gang cleared about $3,300 for the
night. The money was placed in the club
kitty and later on threw a picnic that the
whole city was invited to, which was another
wildly successful venture—though not financially.

"The Superiors finally broke up when
about four of the guys went to jail and a few
others joined the Army.

"All of a sudden, there were only four active members left, and the club had $2,800,
so we did what we thought was best for everyone concerned.

"We voted to split up the treasury. All
right!"

Though "scores" like that were uncommon

for a poor youth from the ghetto, Orenthal
did manage to keep himself in, as he put it,
"lunch money, especially during football season."

He and his pals would head on down to
the 49ers games and sneak in. After enjoying
the game, they went to work.

"The management would give you a nickel
for every seat cushion you turned in.

"Me and my friends would grab all the
cushions we could, and sometimes we'd also
grab all the cushions *other* little dudes had
picked up.

"It was like a *dogfight*," O.J. recalled.

Such antics were fine for a while, but
Orenthal longed for bigger things—and the
way to make real money was to hustle tickets.
For that, a bit of up-front money was required. Orenthal could hustle with the best
of them.

He would go fishing on the pier, and then
sell what he caught in the projects. On Sat-
urdays the pier was too crowded, and so he
would hustle empty bottles for the deposit
money. By game time on Sunday, he usually
had the $3.50 it took to grab a reserved seat
ticket.

"That wasn't to get in, 'cause we'd sneak
in; that was money to work with. Lot's of

times, cats would be waiting for friends who didn't show, and if I thought a guy could be talked out of a ticket, I'd kinda whimper and say, 'Oh, I just *got* to see old Hugh McElhenny.'

"Some people would just give you the ticket, but the average cat would want something for it and he'd say, 'Nope, I won't *give* you the ticket, but how much money you got?'

"You'd tell him $1.50 or two bucks, he'd sell it to you, and then you'd go sell it to somebody else for the $3.50."

When he got really lucky, he catch a ticket for a seat on the 50–yard line. "You could scalp those for four or five bucks."

By game time, Orenthal and his buddies would each pick up around forty dollars. Then it was time to sneak into the stadium.

Simpson, through self-determination and hard work—and a touch of a confidence man—always managed to come out on top, and with a profit.

While in the tenth grade, O.J. Simpson managed to avoid one of the major pitfalls lying in wait to trap modern adolescents. At that period it was the beginning of the counter-culture movement—the Dawning of the Age of Aquarius—which was to lead to free love, increased civil rights for African-Americans, for women, and for gays.

That period in America's cultural history was also to lead to the proliferation of drugs and the psychedelic movement—"the whole Haight-Ashbury thing" as O.J. himself was to put it years later.

"San Francisco always used to have beatniks, but now all these weirdos were coming in from all over the country and the only thing they talked about was *margarine* or *marinara* . . .

"I finally found out it was called marijuana. Up till then, me and my friends thought dope was something you only put in your arm, so we decided to make it over to Haight-Ashbury and see what was happening.

"We'd go down Page and Stanyan Streets and walk into parties and see bald-headed Japanese cats praying and all *kinds* of characters smokin' that shit, and to us, it was just *weird*.

"Naturally the boys had to check out marijuana, and one day at school, we got hold of a joint . . ."

Like a now famous politician, when the joint was passed along to him, young O.J. "just pretended to take a hit."

As he told it later, "I was a diehard athlete, and besides that, I didn't want to get *deranged*, right?"

Finally, there came a time when he couldn't fake it and maintain the adolescent respect of his peers, and so one day he inhaled. He didn't get much out of it. Instead, he ended up running all the way home from school in a total panic, "breathing real hard *to get it out of my system.*

"I believed every horror story I'd heard about grass, and while I was runnin' I remember thinking, 'Goddamn, why did I do that? I'm gonna get addicted!"

That episode effectively ended young Orenthal's experimentation with drugs.

Three

Over school, over his home life, over drugs and social prominence in the closed world of junior high and high school, Orenthal chose sports. O.J.'s first love was baseball, his first dream to be a major-league catcher, and his first hero was Willy Mays. He began to exhibit athletic abilities that belied his earlier medical condition, and became a much sought-after ball player in his neighborhood—the first to be chosen, and the last to be allowed to go home at the end of a long day. He played baseball constantly—leaving school at 3:00, he and his buddies would have their game going by 3:20, a game that would continue, with shifting teams and changing audiences, until 8:30 or 9:00, when it was too dark to continue. He played both baseball, obsessively, and later football, at a government-funded urban youth center called the Potrero Hill Recreation Centre.

"I think I spent more time at the Centre than I did at home or at school," the superstar was to comment years later. The Centre was an important part of his life during these formative years, and to this day O.J. Simpson makes generous donations to the Potrero Hill Recreation Centre, to help them purchase awards and trophies, as well as uniforms for the Centre's athletic teams.

Like a lot of urban African-American youths then and now, Orenthal James Simpson turned to sports as a way out of his situation.

"In the ghetto, everything depends on how good you are at sports," O.J. told *Ebony* magazine in 1976. "I always wanted to be a baseball player. Naturally, Willy Mays was one of my heroes."

When Orenthal was fifteen, he was sent to the Youth Guidance Center in San Francisco—an in-house "incarceration unit"—for about a week. The reason, he says, was a fight he had been involved in, though another account attributes this arrest to his involvement with club members who were caught stealing some bottles from a liquor store.

At the lock-up, he was unimpressed by the lessons authorities tried to teach him, but something happened after he was sent home that was to change his life.

Orenthal expected his father—and his father's belt—to pay him a visit. "I waited in my room, and then I must have dozed off."

The next thing he knew, he was waking up to the sound of voices downstairs.

"Orenthal!" his mother called. "You come here!"

He ran down the stairs. And there, in the living-room of his little house in the slums of San Francisco, sat Willie Mays.

Orenthal had always been a Giants fan, and when the Giants were in town he and a friend would sneak into Seals Stadium—this was before the construction of Candlestick Park—just to see Mays play.

"And there was Willy Mays, waitin' for *me*!"

"You want to come out with me this afteroon?" asked Mays.

Orenthal was astonished. Dumbfounded, the most he could do was nod. At the time, he really didn't know why the baseball great was in his living room—to him, it was some kind of amazing dream; and he didn't want to wake up.

Later, he found out that a youth counselor had gotten word to Mays about a fantastic young athlete who looked like he had just taken a turn down a bad path.

Mays and Orenthal left together, and what the young O.J. remembered the most about this amazing encounter was that instead of a lecture on discipline, Willy Mays treated the star-struck youth as an equal.

They spent the day walking around. Orenthal went with Mays to the cleaners, to the store to buy something, and to someone's house where plans were being made for a banquet.

Mays even took Orenthal to his home.

"He lived in a great big house in Forest Hill," O.J. recalled, "and he was exactly the easygoing, friendly guy I'd always pictured him to be."

They spent the afternoon talking easily. What do you think of the new Chevy? Who's going to win the pennant?

"It was a fantastic day for me," said O.J. "There was nothing serious and never a lecture. It was his way of showing me what to do. He just tried to give me a good example to follow."

After about three hours, Mays drove Orenthal home. To the boy's relief, his father wasn't waiting for him. And, according to O.J., after the Willie Mays day, his father never had cause to whip him again.

"I had an entirely different outlook on ev-

erything after that day with Willie Mays,"
said O.J. "That day with Mays made me realize my dream was possible."

Orethal realized that Mays wasn't superhuman—a quality too often ascribed to gifted
athletes who seem to have superhuman abilities on the playing field. The young athlete
realized that his hero was "an ordinary person." That realization alone made Orenthal
understand something vital.

"I knew there was a chance for me."

Orenthal renewed his determination to become a big-league baseball player.

Unfortunately for his aspirations in that direction, in his sophomore year at Galileo
High School in San Francisco, he broke his
hand. A couple of years later he broke that
same hand again, this time punching out a
neighborhood kid named Donald McGee—
who had a particularly hard head. These two
injuries meant that he couldn't play his beloved baseball for several months at a time.

He turned his athletic prowess in a very
different direction, and by doing so found
two other interests appealing.

"I began to run track, the 100 and 220,
and I noticed all the girls were at the meets,
not at the baseball games.

"That was it for baseball!"

O.J. had no regrets. "I'm not sorry. Baseball is what *could* happen. Football is what *is* happening," the superstar said in 1976, at the pinnacle of his gridiron career.

And it was true. Football became his salvation—a one-way ticket out of the ghetto of Potrero Hill. But it took another revelation like the one he had experienced at the track meets to finally push him in the right direction athletically.

As far as the right direction morally, O.J. would later credit Willie Mays as one of the two key people who helped straighten him out when he was a troubled ghetto youth.

The other person he would credit would be Marguerite Whitley—his first wife.

FIRST LOVES

There's something strangely timeless about life's special moments. Perhaps nowhere is this more true than when a man meets his first love. It's as if lightning strikes and the brilliant flash imprints the details on his mind for the rest of his life.

Dates are forgotten, exact words fade, yet what she wore, how she smiled, the way she made him feel. All of that remains with him through the years, like the ageless images of a snapshot. For some, such a picture is recalled with mixed feelings—sadness, anger, resentment.

The wistful tenderness of those first touches and kisses become clouded with darker images of petty arguments, fading passions, even sudden tragic loss. Eventually, after years of unfulfilled promises, of shattered dreams, feelings may change. Yet somewhere in the mind's eye, a preserved form of that snapshot remains. Because no matter what the years take away, the timeless nature of that picture evokes a wistful recollection of just how powerful, how overriding that first moment was, so long ago, when a man *first* saw his first love.

For Orenthal James Simpson, the first time lightning struck him was in his San Francisco hometown. And, like so many men can also testify when it comes to young love, for O.J., the moment he first saw her was magic.

"She came out of the house," recalled O.J. in an interview years later, "and she had on this white dress, looking like the Virgin Mary or something."

The teenage Marguerite was a sweet, Catholic girl. She was an attractive and charming young woman with an intelligence in her eyes, a genuine warmth to her smile, and a head-turning figure. She caught Orenthal's attention immediately. Not only was Marguerite very pretty, but in the first moment she met him, she would unknowingly turn the tables on her future husband.

When it came to girls, Orenthal was far from shy. He was outgoing and often walked up to any pretty girl and started talking, even if that girl was on the arm of her current boyfriend. Such brazen, even reckless, boldness to go after what he wanted at all cost would become a vital asset in the years to come—and at times, a liability.

Orenthal never thought twice about his brazen aggressiveness, his cocky nature. But he was certainly used to these kinds of moves by now.

What he didn't expect was Marguerite to play the same number on him.

At the time they first met, she was actually dating Orenthal's best friend, Al Cowlings. O.J. and Al grew up together and both played football at Galileo High School. Eventually they would play both college and pro ball together and become lifelong pals—right up to the day Cowlings would risk his life and future for his best friend in the Summer of 1994.

But on this day, Al and Orenthal were simply carefree teenagers, hanging around and having a good time. In fact, Orenthal was happy to give Al a ride over to his girl-friend's home.

Orenthal had borrowed a college re-cruiter's Mustang, and he enjoyed showing it off around the neighborhood. Now, as he sat, lounging in the car in front of Margue-rite's house, his jaw nearly dropped. He watched this vision in white walking right to-ward him. And right *past* her own beau—and his best friend, Al, his *miffed* best friend.

"I sat there thinking, 'Boy *that* is a beau-tiful lady!' " recalled O.J.

A young, aggressive, Orenthal, had just watched the tables turn on him. In that mo-ment, Orenthal the aggressive pursuer, the cocky kid who was always brazenly crossing lines to flirt with other guys' girls had be-come the object pursued.

Now, it was a pretty young woman who had crossed a line, to flirt with *him*!

To Marguerite Whitely, meeting Orenthal presented her with a challenge. She could see his good qualities, his intelligence, his undeniable charm, but she wasn't blind to his rough edges.

In fact, Orenthal's association with gangs, his minor police record, and his reputation on the street, had left Marguerite with the impression that despite his handsomeness and good nature, Orenthal James Simpson was bad news.

"He was really an awful person then," she recalled, acknowledging his charm was hard to resist.

Orenthal and Marguerite became teenage sweethearts. Her stabling influence in his life was a major part of young Orenthal's turn around—away from the streets and toward athletics and a way out of the ghetto. Purpose and focus were gradually becoming a permanent part of his life. Orenthal was beginning to envision his future—and it was bright.

Marguerite Whitely and Orenthal James Simpson would finally marry on June 24, 1967 in a Roman Catholic ceremony.

On their wedding day, Marguerite would walk down the aisle of the church and become yet another beautiful snapshot for her young groom's memories. A lovely June bride—a perfectly realized romantic dream.

Yet the joys of this wedding day would not come about until he'd first realized another great love. This one would first confront him with a challenge and a major disappointment—and this love had nothing to do with romance, but with academics.

Orenthal was in love with the idea of going to the University of Southern California.

"Sometime in 1962 or '63, I was watching the Rose Bowl on television," said O.J. in his 1976 *Playboy* interview. "USC was playing and this dude in a big cape and on a white horse came galloping out on the field.

"I couldn't believe it, and decided right then that that was the school I was going to."

For a boy like Orenthal, who'd already started the race so far behind, the route to his dream university became a symbolic mountain to climb. In fact, for such a ghetto youth, it was a peak so high that no one but a kid with the kind of unique grit, drive, and cocky courage of Orenthal would even come close to reaching it.

Unfortunately, his high school grade point average did not match his ambitions, nor his fierce will, and after he graduated in 1965 he was called up for the draft.

O. J. also told *Playboy* that his grades were bad because "my only interest in school was in gettin' out, so I took courses like home economics and didn't exactly kill myself studying."

A football coach at Arizona State had shown some interest in him, O.J. told *Playboy,* but "he took one look at my grades and told me he'd be in touch when I got out of junior college."

Through this disappointment, and several others in this period, he learned a valuable lesson the hard way. He discovered that in many ways he wasted his youth, and now he was drifting aimlessly. His life lacked focus, and because of that, the only thing he ever wanted, the only thing he ever really cared about, was now denied him.

Instead, the United States military and a small but growing "police action" in Southeast Asia were calling him, as they had called his older brother.

"I was gonna join the Marines and fight in Vietnam, but before I graduated, a friend came back from Vietnam missing a leg, and I thought I had to be *crazy* to go there," said O.J. in an interview years later.

Simpson fooled the draft board by enrolling—at the very last minute—at the City College of San Francisco, a junior college with a small and somewhat successful football team. This move won him a temporary student deferment from the military.

Safe from the draft, and now a big fish in a small pond, O.J.'s athletic abilities were finally showcased. Within a year he was the best player at City College, the envy of his fellow teammates and a much desired escort among the ladies on campus.

For the next two years he struggled in junior college—breaking junior college football rushing records and biding his time, never losing his focus, nor his ambitions to go to USC, which must have seemed as unreachable a goal as ever during this period in his young life.

But O.J., displaying a tenacity that he has demonstrated throughout the course of his athletic career, finally prevailed.

TROJAN TRIUMPHANT

Some offers from universities were made to the junior college gridiron star after his first year. After setting a junior college record in his very first year—a record he extended during his second year there, ending his junior college days with a two-season total of 54 touchdowns at City College of San Francisco— the University of Southern California finally took notice. O.J.'s desire to go there meant that initially he gave up a lot for a promise— and a better shot down the line.

As Simpson told the story in his 1976 *Playboy* interview, CCSF was playing Long Beach in the Prune Bowl. Long Beach was at that time the defending national champion, and after being behind by twenty points in the first half, "we came back and destroyed 'em, 40–20.

"I scored three touchdowns in the second half and was voted Most Valuable Player," he recalled for *Playboy*. "As I was walking off the field, a guy came up to me and said, 'O.J. Simpson, that was a great game. My name is Jim Stangland and I'm a coach at USC. How would you like to be a Trojan?'

"The man had just said the magic word," he told *Playboy*. "Inside my head, *bugles* were blowin' and that white horse was *gallopin'!*"

Unfortunately, after one year of junior college, O.J.'s high school grade point average was still haunting him. It turned out that USC had to see, and would only accept a candidate whose academic improvement covered two years.

"USC couldn't get me in after just one year of junior college. I really didn't want to stay in junior college for another year, but USC assistant coach Marv Goux convinced me I should. So I did . . ." he told *Playboy*.

"He guaranteed me that if I went to USC and played the kind of football he thought I was capable of playing, I'd get more money out of pro football than anybody else ever got—much, much more than any other *school* could offer me."

Thinking ahead, and postponing instant gratification for a bigger payoff down the line, O.J. wisely chose to say no to the other universities, and to stick out yet another year in junior college, for the sake of his dream and the seemingly distant opportunity to go to the University of his choice.

After another record-breaking year in junior college, the big universities really came sniffing.

"That time around, I got a lot of scholarship offers."

In fact, at the time, there was some controversy about the way in which the big universities wooed him and a few other valuable athletes. Several institutions staged a virtual bidding war for O.J.'s services.

"A whole bunch of 'em were offering all kinds of under-the-table shit. In addition to a regular scholarship, most of the schools were talking about $400 or $500 a month and stuff like a car.

"One school was gonna arrange for my mother to clean up an office for $1,000 a month; another was gonna get my mother a house. A lot of stupid Watergate-type recruiting went on in those days."

USC was on the up-and-up and offered nothing under the table.

"It was probably the only school that *didn't*. It was also the only school I'd ever wanted to play for."

ALL-AMERICAN

In the next two years, as the star player on the USC Trojans, O.J. Simpson became an All-American during both of his varsity seasons, and he was to lead the Trojans to a national championship win. In 1968 he swept away a number of N.C.A.A. running records and closed out his undergraduate days by winning the coveted Heisman Trophy, and just about every other major college football awards.

Following his senior year, his coach at USC, John McKay, said of him: "Simpson was not only the greatest player I ever had—he was the greatest player anyone ever had."

The teams he played against never thought such effusive praise was excessive. After watching Simpson zigzag his way for a 150 yard run through a Fighting Irish defensive wall, a Notre Dame sports publicist lamented that, "his nickname shouldn't be Orange Juice. The O.J. should stand for 'Oh, Jesus'— as in 'Oh Jesus, there he goes again!'"

The source of his nickname is the center of some mild controversy in the media during his early days of professional football. Some say that the name sprung from the many lucrative endorsements that came his way—television commercials promoting hired cars and orange juice—hence the nickname, 'The Juice.' Others say that his nickname comes from a period much earlier than that, back to the days when he drank an inordinate amount of orange juice for his early vitamin deficiency.

O.J. himself has clouded the issue, and has told contradictory stories concerning his now-famous nickname.

"A lot of guys probably think I'm *too* active and *too* loud, too *juiced*," he told his 1976 *Playboy* interviewer, "but that's the way I was as a kid."

"But I wasn't called O.J. or Juice when I was little. As a kid I was called Headquarters and Waterhead, because my head was about the same size then as it is now, and I was very sensitive about that."

But O.J. Simpson maintains that it was his professional football days that brought him the title "Juice."

"I've always had lots of energy," he told *Playboy*, "which is why my teammates on the Bills started calling me Juice."

Contrary to what Simpson himself says, it is apparent that he earned the nickname

O.J., Orange Juice or simply "Juice" at least as far back as his days as a Trojan at USC, as the quote from the Notre Dame publicist would indicate. In any case, O.J. shall forever remain "The Juice" to his millions of fans and admirers.

Because he stayed focused on his goal and never sold himself short by going to another of the universities who made him lucrative offers, O.J. Simpson felt that he'd ultimately made the right decision. It was a goal he worked hard for, planned hard to attain, and the payoff, when it came, was glorious.

O.J. loved the University of Southern California, and the university, and the Trojans, loved him.

"I had the time of my life at USC . . . that's where I started getting recognition—and when you're raised in a poor area, that's what you want more than anything else."

O.J. Simpson won every possible award as a college football player—the Heisman Trophy in 1968, he was named the Outstanding College Player of the 1960s Poll, run by the nation's football writers and broadcasters, he was a two-time consensus All-American, and won a host of other honors—and he also established two NCAA records and equalled or bettered no fewer than 13 single season or game records.

And he was an outstanding all-around athlete. He was a member of the world-record-setting 440–yard relay team in college and a member of the 1967–1968 outdoor and indoor national championship track team at Southern California.

Of course, as O.J. Simpson neared graduation, the professional teams were clamoring for him. Suddenly, O.J. Simpson was a marketable commodity.

From ghetto kid to the most valuable athlete of his time, O.J. Simpson was now poised for his biggest grab, a slot on a pro-football team. It was a nearly impossible accomplishment that this hard-driving, obsessive young man nevertheless managed to pull off. In his college years, O.J. Simpson proved to himself and the world that he was a man with athletic talent—and he never, ever sold himself short.

He learned his own value, as an athlete, and later as a movie star and a broadcaster, and he would remain a valuable commodity for the next twenty-five years.

Four

Pro football, as O.J. was to learn, was an entirely different world than the pampered environment of college football, but it was a world he was destined to conquer and dominate, as he had in junior college and at USC.

In junior college, O.J. was very much a big fish in a small pond. At the University of Southern California, he was a whale in a very big pond. But in professional football, he was a much sought after, but as yet unproven commodity.

This fact, however, didn't diminish the size and number of lucrative offers that were made to him by the pros. Yet Simpson knew that he would be required to prove himself once again.

He was starting over.

So, as he did in junior college, as he did when USC asked him to wait one year, and as he did when he finally became a Trojan, he went to work. Work was his salvation.

O.J.'s friends and family knew he always had to be doing something. His aunt, a wise woman who, it is said, had a hand in giving Orenthal his rather unconventional name, used to say he had "ants in his pants."

Playing professional football for a living would satisfy most American men.

Being one of the very best players in history is more than even most professional football players could accomplish—or even hope for.

But it wasn't enough for O.J.

O.J. could *never* do enough. His driven personality, forged when he hustled for money on the streets of Potrero Hill, and when he played on the best college football team of them all in a frantic effort to get out of those streets, would never let him rest.

Make no mistake, football was his life.

But football seasons end. So why not sign a few contracts, do a couple of endorsements? It's more work, more to *do*.

What about those down times, those months when he wasn't on the road, wasn't training?

Sign more contracts. Go on television. Make a few movies between season.

O.J. Simpson did all of these things, and he did them all simultaneously. No sports figure in history ever did more. From star running back, to broadcaster, to movie actor, and back to football in autumn, Simpson was always on the move, always *doing* something.

Such determination borders on obsession.

Running was his life, his vocation. He was the fastest runner there was.

Yet his constant movement on and off the field begs the question: What was he running from?

GREAT PROMISE

Much has been written about Simpson's pro football career. It began in 1969 with the Buffalo Bills, where he became the star running back in his very first season. It ended eleven years later back in his hometown, with the San Francisco 49ers.

His first Bills contract, negotiated by Los Angeles agent Chuck Barnes, was a four-year deal rumored to be worth about $350,000. Everybody thought O.J. Simpson would probably be worth the money. But the key word was *probably*.

Heisman Trophy winners didn't always make the grade in the pros. Like those high school jocks we've all known, the ones who reach the apex of their life in their senior year, and then are forgotten until the high school reunion, Heisman Trophy winners had a habit of peaking early.

It was another pitfall waiting for O.J. to perhaps tumble into. Yet, it became another pitfall that O.J. easily dodged.

O.J. Simpson was an outstanding running back, and he would get even better.

The statistics, the play-by-plays, the career highs and lows are all a matter of record, and have been much lauded and discussed on the sports pages of the daily papers. Also on those pages is the creation of a superstar—because the motor of modern American sports never runs faster and stronger than on the fuel of a player's public image.

We Americans are well aware that we make heroes of our athletes. And heroes have to make an impression that they are superhuman, free of foibles and the all-too-human vices flesh is heir to. O.J. was always aware of this, and so he remained guarded and vigilant to maintain that postive public image.

While other football players went wild on the road, O.J. kept his head.

Drinking binges, womanizing, wrecking bars and hotel rooms, and brawling were not his style.

On the one hand, O.J. felt he had an image to uphold, on the other, he knew this same image was a marketable commodity—just as his athletic ability had been. An untarnished public image could be a financially bankable public image; and for much of his life he did a thorough job of keeping his public and private life separate, and both squeaky clean.

As well as being a workaholic, O.J. Simpson was something of a control freak. These two traits that, until the middle of June, 1994, have kept his head well above the rising floodtides of life.

In the last several decades, we have seen many of our sports legends fall—mass media, the constant scrutiny of every single aspect of their private life—almost always leads to disappointment among the admirers of many sports figures whose feet were revealed to be clay. Our heroes are all-too human.

Rudolph Valentino, the famous silent film star and the biggest box office draw of his time, once said that America builds idols of its heroes so they can tear them down. But too often in the last ten or fifteen years, the professional sports idols have fallen on their own. For every Nancy Kerrigan, there is a

Tonya Harding, for every Roberto Clemente, there is a Vince Coleman.

Our heroes fall, too easily. It is as if, as the twentieth century draws to a close, we are bearing witness to a Wagner-esque Twilight of the Gods.

Such is the case with O.J. Simpson, but two decades ago, when he was at the pinnacle of his athletic career, Simpson displayed the same competence in his personal life as he demonstrated on the athletic field.

Back then, he could do no wrong—both at home, and on the playing field.

As an athlete, to put it bluntly, pro football had never before seen his like. Combining incredible speed with the grace of a gazelle, he has been compared to superstars like the fast and cunning Gale Sayers, and the determined and sturdy Jim Brown.

Not flashy like Joe Namath, Simpson managed to establish himself as the premiere running back of all time, then a successful sports anchor, an actor, and a spokesperson, through quiet determination—or ambitious obsession.

But for a while, people only looked at the athlete.

What they saw impressed them, no matter how cynical the onlookers.

Howard Cosell, the veteran lawyer-turned-sportscaster who was never effusive with his praise, summed up O.J. Simpson perfectly.

"Certainly, O.J. has every skill a truly great running back needs.

"He's got the most spontaneous reflexes of anyone I've ever seen, he has an uncanny ability to lead his blockers and find that extra inch that will allow him to knife through. He seems to have instant acceleration and he also has the strength to break tackles.

"I wouldn't venture to call anyone the greatest running back of all time, because there are too many intangibles involved, but I've never seen any man come to the position with greater gifts."

Though guarded in his praise, as Cosell often was, he nevertheless lavished acclaim on Simpson's athletic performance throughout the superstar's gridiron career.

His fellow players agreed with Cosell's assessment, including the outspoken Jim Brown, the Hall-of-Fame running back whose record O.J. was constantly racing to break.

In his bestselling autobiography *Out of Bounds*, Brown writes "The Juice was fantastic."

"Great running," explained Brown, "is an art so intensely personal, no two men do it quite alike. When a cat makes a beautiful run, it's poetry and jazz. That's why no coach can 'make' a great runner. Great runners are works of God."

Brown included O.J. in his short list of great runners, in addition to other greats: Walter Payton, Gale Sayers, Earl Campbell, and Jim himself, of course.

A massive ego, according to Brown, is also a part of the necessary athletic prowess for a runner.

"Because they're judged by a higher standard, great runners must think, I Am Superior. By the time I walked on the field, I thought, *I* was God. I was the back who would lead the league in rushing. Period. Any Sunday, all I needed was a break, maybe two, and I felt that I would run wild. Don't let anybody kid you . . . all the top runners have felt the same way."

Brown was truly impressed with O.J.'s abilities. "You have to see O.J. out of uniform to appreciate the strength he has in his shoulders," he writes in *Out of Bounds*. "Combined with his world class speed, [and] precise sense of when to accelerate, O.J. was a bitch . . . His ability to run the football matched anyone's."

It was not faint praise, Simpson's accomplishments backed Brown's assessment.

His National Football League records include, of course, the most rushing yards ever gained in a single season—2,003 yards, a 1973 feat which broke Jim Brown's record, a record which stood for over a decade.

"When I broke Jim Brown's record for yards gained in one season," recalled O.J. in an interview eleven years after that 1973 feat, "he went out of his way to point to Franco Harris and say, 'Now there's a great football player.'"

Such a slight must have stung O.J.

But then again, to the fiercely competitive Brown and Simpson, much of this was more grist for the ego mill.

"I'm sure Jimmy never expected his record to be broken," quipped O.J. in that 1984 interview, zinging a public barb he'd been holding back for eleven years.

Conversely, in 1977, when Walter Payton broke O.J.'s rushing record of 273 yards in one game—Payton rushed for 275 yards—O.J. took the high road. Perhaps recalling Brown's stinging comment about Franco Harris, Simpson made sure to congratulate the Chicago Bears star.

Ironically, Pittsburgh Steeler Franco Harris

along with Walter Payton *would* run to break Brown's total rushing record while O.J. would not.

No matter. During his pro career, there would be other records for O.J. to break:

After shattering Brown's season rushing record, O.J. broke the record for most rushing yards gained in a single game—250.

Then he broke the record for most touchdowns in a single season—23.

He held many of these records for a number of years, and his record of most rushing yards in a single season still stands.

By 1976, he was fourth on the NFL's list of all-time ground gainers, and by the end of that year he moved up to second place, though he never managed to eclipse Jim Brown's NFL lifetime record of 12, 312 yards. Even though injuries sidelined him for two out of his eleven seasons with the pros, he came very close.

Why didn't O.J. crack Brown's mark?

The two years of sidelining injuries was one reason; his coaches' fears of losing him to injury was another. O.J. was such a valuable commodity that coaches used him somewhat sparingly during his first three years as a pro. Those were vital years that would have added valuable yardage to his lifetime total.

But how did O.J. Simpson really feel about never breaking Jim Brown's lifetime rushing record?

Near his retirement from pro ball, O.J. gave the impression that records didn't mean much to him. When asked about the records he failed to break, his response was a simple one:

"I can live without them."

At that time, O.J. said he felt he had broken enough records.

When he was asked about his own rushing record—2,003 yards in the 1973 season—he was philosophical about it standing, though still proud:

"Oh, the record will be broken, the way records are," he told *Ebony* magazine in September, 1981. "But," he added, "being the first, can never be taken away . . . that 2,000 yards put me in football's lore."

A few years later, however, working as a commentator for Monday Night Football and anticipating a nomination within the year to the NFL Hall of Fame, a 37–year-old O.J. would change his tune about the meaning of those records.

According to a 1984 *Jet* magazine article, O.J. revealed that he felt he should have been the first to break Jim Brown's rushing record instead of Chicago Bears star Walter Payton.

"In what are the best years of an athlete's life," he explained, "mine were wasted running pass patterns. All I really needed was a coach who understood running the ball and I would have had 14,000 yards [instead of 11,236 yards] by the time I retired," said Simpson.

O.J. played for a total of seven coaches during his sports career, but the coach who O.J. is most likely to agree wasted his running talent was his first pro coach.

John Rauch coached the Buffalo Bills during O.J.'s first years on the team. Rauch ascribed to the notion that O.J., Rauch's No. 1 draft choice, could not carry the load he'd had in college.

"I couldn't build my offense around one back, no matter how good he is," said Rauch, according to a 1973 *Sports Illustrated* article. "That's not my style."

Rauch was concerned that using O.J. as a runner to any great extent would make it too easy for the opposing team to set up defensive keys. He chose instead to use this gifted runner as a pass receiver.

"We expect him to block, too," said Rauch in the same interview, essentially explaining away one more reason why O.J. failed to accomplish a feat most sports analysts agree that he had been more than capable of.

Yet, no matter the records, or how O.J. really felt about them standing years later, his was truly an outstanding Hall-of-Fame career. It inked him permanently onto the books and into the memories of the millions of fans who watched with sheer pleasure the glory and the beauty of his playing.

It was O.J.'s destiny, it seemed, to become one of the most highly-paid, most accomplished, and most recognized, athletes of his day.

THE MAKING OF A HERO

O.J. was also destined to be one of the most loved athletes of his generation, and, at the time he was being wooed by the pro football teams, O.J. was near the peak of his physical prowess.

He cut an imposing figure. Those who met him face-to-face were—and still are—often surprised that he was slightly better looking that even the photographs suggest, and in pictures he always "cut a dashing figure," as Italian actress Sophia Loren said of him years later, when she worked with O.J. on the filming of *The Cassandra Crossing.*

At six-foot-one, and weighing in at a lean 212 pounds, Simpson was the consummate athlete, enjoying amateur track, tennis and basketball as well as his career in pro football. His friend, Bill Withers, while taking pokes at O.J.'s singing ability—"O.J. has a distinctive sound, but who wants to hear a foghorn try to warble ballads?"—spoke positively about Simpson's affable and charming personality.

"He can walk into a room and suddenly everyone in it is smiling and feeling amiable . . . O.J. seems to make people glow as opposed to, say, Warren Beatty, who immediately gets people wondering if their sex lives are all they should be."

Withers went on to speak about that special bond that Simpson had with his friends.

"People who know O.J. rave about his easy, up-front good humor, and I certainly didn't detect any chinks in the armor."

Others speak about Simpson in similar terms.

But it seems that O.J. Simpson went through a lot of trouble to keep any "chinks" hidden from the public eye.

* * *

Buffalo, New York, likes to call itself the "Queen City of the Lakes," a rather ironic title to bestow on a rusty and depressed blue-collar city ravaged by unemployment in the late 1960s, a situation that only worsened throughout the decade of the '70s.

A frozen city in the winter—with colder average temperatures than much of the rest of New York state—Buffalo thaws out in the summer to become a place of dirty acid rain, industrial grime, industrial parks, and soot.

Although the people of Buffalo are a warm, hard-working, down-to-earth lot, the weather was far from a welcome change to Californians like the Simpson family, used to much balmier temperatures year round.

It's a bitter place to attend a football game. On one NFL season opening day—the season of 1975—the winds from Lake Erie, three miles away, were so cold, bitter, and fierce, that they reached gale force proportions.

The home team was nothing special, certainly not the team of the decade—that honor went to the Pittsburgh Steelers, whose much-vaunted "Steel Curtain" was to take them to Super Bowl victory after victory in the mid-1970s—but what the Bills lacked in overall talent, they made up for in the caliber of their star player.

O.J. Simpson was that star, and he became
their star almost overnight, in his very first
season with Buffalo.

Yet, things didn't look so promising in the
beginning.

Simpson had a rude awakening in store for
him when he arrived in Buffalo. He'd been
an outstanding player at USC, and everything there was first class—from the locker
rooms to the stadium. But the Bills were a
poor team with a losing record, and that pov-
erty-row mentality was reflected in the condition in which the players trained, traveled,
and worked.

The hometown facilities were incredibly
bad, and the Bills were a team that actually
liked to play away games. War Memorial Stadium "had to be seen to be believed," according to Simpson.

"When I first saw it, I *didn't* believe it."

At USC in Los Angeles, O.J. played in the
Los Angeles Coliseum, a graceful and impressive deco structure which can be seen
gleaming whitely from miles away. It is an
architectural wonder, and a thing of beauty.

In Buffalo, you walked through some
pretty bad neighborhoods—"black neighborhoods," O. J. was to point out to a reporter
with ironic horror—then you rounded a cor-

ner, and there it was. Fifty feet in front of you there squatted a ramshackle, aging stadium that could double for some of the larger high school stadiums on the West Coast—except for the fact that it was much too dilapidated.

The practice locker rooms were located, not in the "stadium" proper, but in a nearby public ice rink. And the locker room was shared with kids getting ready for high school hockey games.

Team meetings were conducted in the hallway of the ice rink, right around the refreshment machines. The assistant coaches strung wires and hung blankets right before the meetings so that no one would wander in.

"While we'd be going over game plans, kids would come through to get ice cream and sodas. That seemed a little strange," Simpson confessed.

"I found the Bills to be rinky-dink."

What he saw of the Bills when he got to Buffalo was a long, far cry from the guts-and-glory, glamourous image the young Simpson had come to associate with the "pros."

Simpson became very much of a public figure by 1969—for not only was he an unequalled football player—he didn't wait long to branch out into other fields of endeavor.

On September 19, 1969, ABC Sports signed the gridiron star to a long-term broadcasting contract, which meant that by the end of his *first year* of pro football, he became a national television and radio personality.

ABC executives fairly gushed, issuing a press release that read in part:

"Versatile football phenomenon O.J. Simpson has signed a long-term contract with ABC Sports, Inc. to become an ABC television and radio personality at the end of the upcoming pro football season, it was announced today by Roone Arledge, President of ABC Sports.

Arledge, with an instinct for talent that was unparalleled, realized Simpson's drawing power and his prodigious talents.

"O. J. Simpson is one of the most versatile young men in sports," said Arledge in the press release, "not only as an athlete but as a well-informed and articulate spokesman for athletics. We think he has the potential to develop over the years into an outstanding broadcast personality—whether it be as a sports show host, a sports commentator or even as an actor.

"O.J. has said he would like a career in

television when his playing days are done and ABC feels he has the long range potential to become successful in this endeavor."

ABC grabbed Simpson quickly, just as Buffalo did, effectively beating out the competition.

The contract that Simpson signed provided ABC Sports with the exclusive rights to Simpson's services as a sports broadcaster on both radio and television, and made provisions for the celebrity's appearances on the top sports show in the history of broadcasting, "ABC's Wide World of Sports."

O.J. effectively became their pre- and post-season football program commentator—of course, he was busy on the playing field *in* season—and he also appeared on news programs on the ABC television network, and even managed to make an appearance on several of ABC's entertainment programs.

Simpson was also contracted to appear on one or more of the network-owned local television stations, and even on ABC network radio.

It was stipulated that the ABC contract would not interfere with O.J.'s professional football career—at that time he was only a rookie with the Buffalo Bills and had a reputation to build—and, though details have never been revealed, the contract was said to be one of the most lucrative ever offered to a current or former athlete moving into broadcasting.

Such a generous and exclusive offer, especially to what amounted to an unproven commodity, was totally unheard of before this. The news caused something of a sensation in the broadcasting world, and some in the television business no doubt thought that Roone Arledge had lost his marbles.

Of course, the naysayers were proven wrong. O.J. Simpson's contracts were extended—with only a brief jump to NBC—through 1986. He went on to become a familiar and vital member of the broadcasting team on "Monday Night Football," and he joined Frank Gifford and Joe Namath in announcing almost a hundred Monday night and weekend games, not to mention a side-trip to the Olympics.

But O.J. never forgot what got him into the broadcast booth and on national television—his abilities on the playing field.

It was an incredible rookie year for "The Juice"—winning both the most valuable player with the Buffalo Bills, and an unprecedented broadcasting contract.

From that auspicious beginning, Simpson's

sports career really took off. In his fifth year as a pro, he broke the all-time season rushing record, which proved to be his most impressive accomplishment, and the most durable—it is still on the record books.

Though he never won a Super Bowl, he took the Bills to victory after victory in season after season, as well as winning fans in the broadcasting arena when football season was over.

His fellow teammates in Buffalo both loved and respected Simpson, and he, in turn, treated them all with respect and affection. He was fiercely competitive, but he covered his aggressive streak with affable good humor. He had a sense of humor and was something of a prankster—and a hustler.

Simpson, as some members of the Bills learned, was a bit of a card shark. "He'll cheat you at cards if you turn your eyes," warned All-AFC defensive back Robert James, who joined the Bills the same year as O.J.

"He'll look in your hand. He doesn't think that's wrong; he's just so competitive.

"If he's caught, it's comical to him; he'll laugh."

A profile of "The Juice", published in a 1973 issue of *Sports Illustrated*, offers a por-

trait of the O.J. Simpson that played for Buffalo in those early years.

"Friends are fond of saying that [Simpson]
is just a regular guy," that 'his hat size has
never changed.' 'The Juice' wears a perpet-
ual smile; frequently laughing in his deep
baritone. He is a man of unlimited good nature whose disposition resembles that of his
mother's first cousin, Ernie Banks."

Buffalo Bills owner, Ralph Wilson, said of
his most valuable player, "O.J.'s a better person than he is a football player, if that's possible."

The instigator in a couple of pranks, he
was also the butt of several pranks staged by
his teamates. One time O.J.'s best friend and
Buffalo Bill's teammate, Al Cowlings, a 255–
pound bear of a defensive end, won $100
from Simpson on a mile race by actually
beating him.

It happened during training camp. Simpson had been physically working very hard
that day, and Cowlings—even as big and slow
as he was—believed he had a good chance of
beating the fleet-of-foot running back who'd
been his best friend since childhood.

O.J. scoffed as he took up the wager. He
even made a big show of how little effort it

would take to win a foot race against Cowlings.

But, to his own stunned surprise—like the hare watching the tortoise cross that finish line—O.J. lost.

"O.J. was pooped out," another teamate explained. "When your pooped some say you got the monkey on your back, some say you got the bear. Well, O.J. had an elephant!"

Looking back, O.J. admitted that he "almost" had Cowlings "psyched." His plan had been to let Cowlings get a little ahead and then pull up alongside him. "I was going to laugh and say, 'Wanna quit?'" But O.J. never got the chance.

Cowlings pulled away and lightened his best friend of a one-hundred dollar bill.

It was not the first time O.J. Simpson and Al Cowlings would race together, and it wouldn't be the last. Cowlings and O.J. had forged a fast friendship from their days on Potrero Hill to playing football together in high school.

In fact, Cowlings seemed to be in lockstep with O.J. for much of their early careers. After high school, Cowlings joined O.J. at San Francisco City College and then at the University of Southern California.

Both Cowlings and O.J. were even first

round draft picks—one year apart—for the Buffalo Bills. They played together during the early 1970s until their paths split and Cowlings was traded to Houston, then later played for the Los Angeles Rams.

Ironically, their career paths reunited again when both were nearing retirement from pro-ball. Both played for the San Francisco 49ers, back in the hometown where it all started.

That training camp race foreshadowed another, much stranger one in the years to come when the entire nation would watch in shock and stunned horror as these best friends raced through the streets of Los Angeles. In the summer of 1994, Cowlings would be driving a white Ford Bronco, his childhood friend, O.J., in the back with a gun as dozens of police cruisers paced behind them.

It would be a shocking and terrible race, on the heels of two shocking and tragic murders; a race that would lead them into a future filled with uncertain consequences.

Five

O.J. emerged from his first five years of pro football as one of the most-liked athletic figures in American sports. Off season, he was on television and radio constantly, in season, he was a perennial gridiron star and record breaker.

As his fame grew, so did his legend, and his legion of fans—fans he never turned away.

O.J. spent more than his share of time on the charity circuit, and he always insisted on keeping himself especially accessible to young fans—no doubt due to his fond memory of that day spent with Willy Mays years before.

Simpson was a man who did not forget where he came from. He adopted the Potrero Hill Recreational Centre, where he spent much of his time as a teenager As a pro, he donated time and money for their continuing expenses.

In addition, O.J.'s humanitarian efforts extended to the New York State Cancer Crusade, where he served as the honorary chairman.

His work boosting boys' clubs and summer camps for the disadvantaged became evidence of a man who believed in giving back something after getting so much.

He won favor from sports journalists—not always the most sympathetic people in the world—as well as from his fellow players.

Among his teammates, he was something of a legend. As a superstar who could easily overshadow his fellow players, O.J. instead reached out to them. He took the time to praise—quite publicly—their efforts and accomplishment.

While playing for Buffalo in those early years, O.J. insisted that his fellow Bills were as much the cause of his career successes as he was.

Simpson repeatedly focused his praise and attention on his blockers. Consequently, the attention of journalists and broadcasters also fell that way, and as a result, previously neglected players like Reggie McKensie, Joe DeLamielleure, Mike Montler, Dave Foley and Dominic Green were able to win media attention—and generous salary increases—on their own merit as the phenomenal "Electric Company."

Simpson's appreciation of the blockers efforts carried over to their personal relationship. Following the 1973 season, the year he broke the season rushing record, Simpson presented members of the coaching and offensive team with over $20,000 worth of personalized gold bracelets—emblazoned with the number 2,003 (the amount of yards rushed to break the record) and signed "Juice."

It was a generous gesture he could well afford because of the fact that his football salary alone reached $300,000 in that year. And that was not counting his pay from ABC Sports and the many financially-lucrative promotional deals he signed.

With his fans in Buffalo, and with his first couple of pro football coaches, his relationships were a little more problematical.

Simpson had always had something of a troubled relationship with the Buffalo fans. In the beginning, he got booed a lot.

The reason:

"Because we weren't winning. When I got to Buffalo, I was supposed to be the kid from California who was gonna instantly turn things around for the Bills.

". . . there was no way that could happen."

Part of the problem, according to Simpson

and several other players on the Bills, was coach John Rauch.

Rauch has a reputation of being inflexible, stubborn and something of a control fanatic. Simpson said of him that he was the kind of guy who, "once he says something, will stick with it no matter what—which I think worked against him in Buffalo." Simpson added, rather guardedly, "I know it worked against me."

Rauch seemed to have it in for Simpson. When O.J. reported to Buffalo, he was an eager, bright-eyed rookie, a Heisman Trophy winner with stars in his eyes.

John Rauch tried to make O.J. a receiver instead of using him for what he did best—playing as the team's running back. Because Simpson was a rookie, he didn't have the confidence to speak up.

That situation did not last long. As O.J.'s confidence grew, he began to run head-to-head with Rauch. By the time Simpson's second year came around, it was clear to him that Rauch's strategy was a failure and it was time for a change.

Rauch, threatened by an upstart rookie, stuck to his losing guns. It got pretty hot between the rookie and the coach that year.

"About as hot as it could get," was how O.J. typified their rocky relationship.

"I still take pride in the fact that I never asked to be traded during those years, but believe me, there were times I just wanted to scream and get out of there," Simpson confessed to a reporter a few years later.

But O.J. stuck it out, mostly because of another man in the Bills organization, a public relations executive by the name of Jack Horrigan, who at that time was suffering from incurable leukemia.

"Jack was dying of leukemia, but at moments when I was ready to bail out, he'd come around and comfort *me*."

Simpson got emotional whenever he spoke about Jack Horrigan in the years that followed.

" 'Juice,' " he'd say, 'there are times in your life when stuff like this is gonna happen, and you just have to ride it out. Things'll get better.'

"When things did get better, Jack had unfortunately passed away."

Another reason O.J. stayed with the Bills was because of a knee injury early in his pro career. In the eighth game of his second year, Simpson got hit really hard returning a kick-off against Cincinnati. His left knee

took the brunt of the impact and he was
through for the season. Fortunately, that also
meant he was far away from his nemesis,
John Rauch.

When he came back in the beginning of
the next season, Rauch was fired and replaced by Harvey Johnson.

Of Johnson, Simpson felt he was "a great
guy but certainly not a man qualified to be
a head coach."

Simpson's opinion of Johnson's skill as a
coach was borne out by the fact that the Bills
won exactly one game that whole season.

In sum, O.J. led the Bills in rushing in
each of his first three years of pro ball. During his first season, Buffalo won four games.
That winning total dwindled down to three
the next year; and finally there was that awful season of only one win. In contrast, while
the Bills record diminished, O.J. gained 697,
488, and 742 yards, respectively.

"I was playing the game but not enjoying
it," he admitted of those first years in a 1973
Sports Illustrated article.

This was a low point for O.J.

"O.J. Simpson. Remember?" wrote Edwin
Shrake in a 1971 *Sports Illustrated* article.
"Big, graceful guy in a red and gold uni-
form. Used to carry the ball 30, 40 times a

game for USC. Nearly always made 100 yards, sometimes 200. Tremendous drive, 9.4 speed, tough enough to take the shots and come right back. Alltime All-American. Won the Heisman Trophy. Going to be All-Pro as sure as a wolf will eat a chicken. So what happened?

"He went to Buffalo and disappeared in a snowbank, maybe with just his shoes sticking out, and people would come by and say, 'I think that's O.J. in there, but I don't see enough of him to know for certain.'"

After his glorious days at USC, O.J. had signed a number of lucrative business contracts. But after three years on a team with a dismally diminishing record, those contracts were beginning to expire, and O.J. was beginning to wonder if the glory was over.

What would happen to his future?

Pondering that question, O.J. reportedly took a long steamship trip early in his third year, 1971. A fan sent him a ticket to Africa. While there he did much soul searching, returning with the announcement that he had decided to play only five years as professional football player.

But something would happen to change O.J.'s future—or rather some*one*. A new Bills' coach named Lou Saban.

PERSONAL BEST

Lou Saban was a coach well-remembered in Buffalo. In the mid-1960's Saban had led the Bills to victory and the winning of two straight AFL championships.

O.J. suspected Saban was a man who would allow O.J. to run some record-breaking yardage. In fact, the previous season, when O.J. had managed to run 742 yards, only one player had beat him, a player named Floyd Little, who had played for Saban at Denver.

"We had about the same average," remarked O.J., "but Floyd had 100 more carries, and I think the more you carry, the better your average gets."

That is exactly what O.J. was hoping would happen under Saban's leadership with the Bills.

O.J. got a look at Saban's playbook in the 1972 training camp. After that, O.J. was convinced. Even though his old contract with the Bills still had a year to run out, O.J. decided at that point to gamble on remaining with this underdog team. He could only hope that Saban would finally use his player's extraordinary running talents to the benefit of the entire team.

O.J. signed a new multiple-year contract.

As he put it, "I've cried with these guys. Now I want to drink champagne with them."

O.J.'s hunch to trust Saban had been a good one.

With the opening of the 1973 season, Saban announced his plan to essentially pull the Bills up through the strengths of Simpson. As Saban saw it, a player like O.J. was the hub of a wheel, around which the other players became spokes.

"All the talking in the world is of no consequence: you need examples and you want to use a man to set high standards who's capable of reaching them."

To Saban, O.J. had reached those high standards before, and he would see to it that the young player would reach them again.

"I'm going to get quality linemen to block for you," Saban promised O.J. And he did. Guards Reggie McKenzie (6 foot 2 inches, 244 pounds), and Joe Delamielleure (6 foot 5 inches, 247 pounds); Tackles Donnie Green (6 foot 7 inches, 252 pounds), and Dave Foley (6 foot 5 inches, 247 pounds); and at center, Mike Moniter (6 foot 4 inches, 245 pounds).

"From Saban's very first day," said Dick

Cunningham, a Bill's tackle and linebacker, "O.J. was our offense."

At the start of the season, in the very first game against New England, O.J. set a league record for a single game when he rushed for 250 yards.

The Hall of Fame requested his jersey (NO. 32) and two times within the first four weeks he was named AP Offensive Player of the Week.

The Bill's blockers became known as the "Electric Company" because they were the ones who turned on "The Juice."

O.J. would keep behind the line while his excellent blockers worked and then instantly accelerate when the hole showed in the opponent's defense. Then O.J.'s uncanny sense of the field would drive to bob and weave, cut and fake, and finally to run. O.J. would soon be gaining enough yardage to begin breaking records.

By December 1973, an entire nation of football fans turned their attention to a frigid Shea Stadium. There, in a game between the New York Jets and the Buffalo Bills, football history was going to be made.

"Hey, man," a Shea Stadium functionary confided to a Buffalo Bill on the snowy sidelines at the December game, "the Juice still needs three yards."

"Four," corrected the Bill.

On the next play, according to a *Sports Illustrated* rundown, with four minutes and 26 seconds remaining the first quarter, O.J. Simpson saw blocks from the left side of his line and churned through the snow for six yards to break Jim Brown's 10-year-old National Football League single season rushing record of 1,863 yards.

The 47,740 shivering fans rose to their feet to applaud the running back as the referee stopped the game to ceremoniously hand Simpson the ball. "The Juice" toted the recently christened relic to the sidelines for safekeeping.

"More, Juice, more," chanted his teammates, "Let's get more," they urged, as Simpson lazily jogged back to the huddle.

And there would be more. With 5:56 remaining in the game, Simpson burst out of the line for seven yards to the New York 13-yard line. That seven yards was what finally did it.

O.J.'s teammates rushed onto the field and lifted him onto their shoulders. "The Juice" had done it, he'd surpassed an unthinkable distance in one season—2,000 yards!

What seemed to amaze *Sports Illustrated* writer Ron Fimrite, as well as the thousands of fans, was that O.J. did it in the conditions that day:

"What is perhaps most remarkable about Simpson's record spree," wrote Fimrite, "is that it was made possible by two games played on fields of such Siberian frigidity they were fit only for eluding wolves.

"While teammates and foes alike were battling futiley to gain purchase on the frozen tundra; Simpson . . . traversed the snowcaps as swiftly and as surely as an avenging Cossack."

In that one game, Simpson had exceeded the legendary Jim Brown's record for both yardage gained and for most carries in a season.

To O.J., who ironically wore Brown's old number 32, this was the fulfillment of another very special dream—this one just as bold and brazen as his childhood dares.

Jim Brown first remembered meeting O.J. when Simpson was an All-American and a Heisman Trophy winner at USC in the late '60s. But O.J. remembers another meeting, this one much earlier.

"Well, you know how kids are. We started fooling around, mumbling things, and finally, I just walked right up to him and said, 'Mr.

Brown, someday I'm going to break all your records, wait and see.'

"I know it sounds unbelievable now," O.J. told a reporter in 1973, "but I was just kidding around."

According to O.J., Brown hardly looked at the young Simpson. "He just kind of walked away, smiling. Now that we've gotten to know each other, I felt I could ask him if he remembered that time. Naturally he didn't remember it at all. Why should he? Just some dumb kid."

Not anymore.

Jim Brown praised O.J. Simpson's running talent. In his book, *Out of Bounds,* Brown made clear that being a running back is no easy task. Speeding down the field with the ball, a good back cannot worry about the 250 pound tackle barreling toward his valuable legs. He who hesitates, as a back, is truly lost.

"O.J. the runner was the genuine item," admitted Brown in his book. He also had a few nice moves, but he wasn't pretty like he says he was . . .

"The Juice didn't have to be pretty. His ability to run the football matched anyone's. It's not what he's noted for, but O.J. ran with great determination. Though he wasn't punishing, the Juice *was* going forward, and there would be no hesitation before a hit. At his best, O.J. had a lot of heart.

"When I talk about backs, I talk about heart a lot. When you're running the football, you better at least have some. Some backs lack talent yet they're brave. Others have gifts but not the courage. The man with great skill and great heart is devastating. He will kick your ass a lot."

"O.J. senses tacklers," said linebacker Dick Cunningham, who played with O.J. in Buffalo before heading to the Houston Oilers. "He makes cuts that are uncanny. It's almost like the guy coming up behind him is yelling, 'Here I come. You better go the other way.' "

O.J. explained that he wasn't psychic, he was just very good at reading telegraphed movement. No matter how low the mercury dropped in Buffalo—and it would drop plenty—O.J. would always be seen on the field wearing a short-sleeved jersey, exposing bare arms.

"I can feel the tackles better that way," he explained. "I can feel their touch, and in a football game, I just don't want to be touched. The more I feel that way, the better the game I play."

Of course, it always helped that O.J. would

be able to shift to top speed from a standstill and hit that speed after only two strides.

O.J. insisted that his talents were instinctive. He even told sports reporters that he felt like he was a better runner when he was tired because he thought less and simply reacted.

As linebacker Cunningham agreed, the characteristic that most distinguished O.J. Simpson from other backs was his extraordinary sense of where he is on the field and what, and who was around him.

Sportswriters began to pick up the vernacular for O.J.'s amazing weaving and bobbing at full speed, which soon became known as "the juke" and the "okey-doke."

Now you see him. Now you don't!

"Don't try for the big hit on O.J.," said Don Shula, coach of the Miami Dolphins, warning his tacklers of the unstoppable 'Juice'. "O.J.'s got such great moves you'll grab only air. Just try to get a piece of him, then wait for help."

In 1973, the Head Coach of the Philadelphia Eagles, Mike McCormack, reportedly said he would like to have O.J.'s eyes tested because he seemed to "sense" tacklers he couldn't possibly see.

Back at USC, Coach John McKay used to

marvel at Simpson's ability to recall the blockers and potential tacklers who figured in his long runs.

According to Simpson's philosophy, "good backs" would not get blind-sided. To prepare himself, he would watch the reactions of all defenders in game films. In any given situation O.J. said he could envision relatively accurately the position of any player who might have an opening to tackle him.

All the hard work, all the battles through the frustrating coaching and painful injuries had finally paid off for O.J. Simpson on that cold December day.

The Bills would close out the 1973 season with a 9–5 record, their best in seven years. And O.J. would close the season as a record-breaking hero.

He was back on top. And just as he said he would earlier in the season, he was finally drinking champagne with his teammates.

Two seasons later, alchemist O.J. Simpson had helped transform owner Ralph Wilson's Buffalo Bill's lackluster franchise into solid gold.

O.J. was on top of the world by 1975. That December he was first runner up for the

"*Sports Illustrated* Sportsman of the Year" award, but first prize that year went to baseball player Pete Rose, who was later to lose it all, and his shot at making baseball's Hall of Fame, in a gambling scandal.

At the time of this award, Simpson spoke of his self-confidence and his pride in becoming the best.

"I am more satisfied a player now than I've ever been—I'm at my peak physically and mentally, I know what I have to do, the way it should be done, without having to prove myself or satisfy my pride—and vanity—the way I did when I was younger.

"It doesn't bother me as much when I don't get the ball."

His career was at its height, but for O.J. Simpson and his wife Marguerite, all was not well at home.

O.J. Simpson lost much of his youthful naive joy of athletic competition by 1975, he was mature, but just as he was hitting his personal best, problems at home and even a few professional problems began to plague him. Though always careful about his public image, things began to go very wrong by the middle of the 1970s, and people began learning things about O.J.'s life in the fast lane.

The first thing to go astray was O.J. Simpson's little-publicized marriage, to his high school sweetheart, a marriage which ended for good in 1979, and was not without deep personal tragedy along the way.

Six

Marguerite Whitney met the superstar under less that auspicious circumstances. He wasn't a superstar yet, nor even a particularly noted athlete. When O.J. Simpson meet Marguerite, he was just a high school junior, a street kid from the neighborhood around Potrero Hill, know by a couple of street names—"Waterhead," "Motormouth," "Headquarters."

They were an interesting couple from the first, and some of their acquaintances from that time thought their romance . . . well, strange.

O.J. was always brash and outgoing, a street kid who was always hustling. It seemed odd to see him dating Marguerite, a little shy, she was really a quiet person, though she carried herself proudly and conveyed a special kind of dignity.

Many have spoken of O.J.'s striking good looks, few speak of Marguerite's overpowering beauty. "She has a spiritual beauty, and a special kind of aura," said one longtime associate who wished to remain anonymous.

In truth, Marguerite is an attractive African-American woman, tall, with an impressive figure and warm, genuine smile. She is every inch a woman, and some of their mutual friends say she's the one with the brains, O.J. provides the drive and the determination, and the "street smarts."

Privately, some thought that O.J. and Marguerite Whitney had married too soon, that O.J. got married to a woman who would never share his interests, his obsessive workaholism, his towering ambitions.

They met in California, and, even during his years with the Bills, she would remain a California girl—traveling no further with her husband than to Berkley, and later to Bel Air. Marguerite was constantly refusing many offers by the Bills management to come and make her home in the forbidding climate of Buffalo.

Marguerite liked the California climate, and the year-round swimming—her favorite pastime, and one she shared with her children.

High school sweethearts, Marguerite followed her man to junior college, and then on to the University of Southern California. Like her husband, though with less relish for the role, Marguerite became the sophisticated cosmopolitan. It was this cosmopolitanism that kept O.J. from moving permanently to Buffalo, a town he considered dull.

For Marguerite, it was the weather and her family that kept her in California. She preferred to stay close to her roots—and perhaps she also preferred remaining with her children in a much better neighborhood and in a much more exciting city.

They married quite young, O.J. was nineteen and Marguerite was eighteen. Simpson later admitted that they both had "a lot of growing up to do."

Marrying this young is often a recipe for disaster, but, at least in 1976, O.J. was singing its praises. He spoke about his marriage to a reporter at that time.

"I wouldn't advise it for everybody, but for me it was probably the best thing.

"I was pretty extroverted and I did a lot of messing around, and marriage sort of gave me some responsibility at an age when I needed it.

"I stayed home nights with my wife—she was working so she was usually too tired to go out—and did my homework.

"If I hadn't been married and had her to go home to, I think I could have been moving a little too fast for myself."

Simpson had a sensible philosophy toward marriage, but sensible philosophies often fall by the wayside when confronted with harsh realities.

"All my life, I'd always visualize myself as a father, with kids, but I never really thought about being a husband, and there are certain responsibilities you have as a husband. That's hard for a free spirit like me," he told the journalist in 1976.

"Fortunately, I've got a good lady and she's made adjustments for it."

This statement could be taken as a tacit admission that O.J. has had a few flings on the road, but he remained guarded in his statements about this facet of his personal life.

"I haven't run into a plethora of groupies," he laughed.

He later told an interviewer that, as far as marriage goes, it really "all comes down to the two of us, how much we love each other.

"We've had our problems, like any other couple, probably a few more of them, because of my lack of privacy."

That lack of privacy, as well as the seven or eight-month separations in a given year—during football season and because of his broadcasting career, weighed heavily on their marriage.

As Simpson told an interviewer in 1976, "Marguerite wasn't happy in Buffalo; she just didn't have much to do." Her stubbornness and his career commitments conspired to keep them apart more than they were together.

With his wife on the West Coast, and O.J. on the East Coast, it was inevitable that a strain was put on their marriage. And even when football season was over, the strain continued.

"When football is over for the year, it seems like I'm always on the road, making appearances for the companies I work for . . . All that keeps me on the road and has led to a lot of trouble for us.

"Marguerite and I were apart more than we were together and a marriage can't work when you're separated so much of the time."

Candid about his personal life in 1976, Simpson admitted that the fundamental problem "boils down to a question of my family versus playing football away from home again."

That problem came to a head that year, when O.J. Simpson demanded to be traded to a West Coast team. As the football season loomed, and no trade was imminent, O.J. sent out an ultimatum.

"TRADE ME, OR I'M THROUGH!"

If he wasn't traded, he would quit football for life.

It was a decision that rocked the sports world and threatened to demoralize the Buffalo Bills, but it hurt Simpson as well, perhaps more deeply than he first realized.

In the September 27th issue of *Newsweek*, Pete Axthelma talked to Simpson about his decision to give that ultimatum of "trade me or I'm through."

Axthelma found the superstar glumly contemplating retirement from a game that had done so much for him in the past, that was such a vital part of his life.

"The deal had not taken place, and O.J. seemed restless and disappointed," Axthelma wrote. It seemed O.J. could be doomed to live up to his own ultimatum and stay out of football.

Simpson told the reporter that "movie people were pressing me for commitments of my time, legal people wanted me to sue to break my contract, but I didn't want to end my career, and I certainly didn't want to end it in a courtroom."

Simpson was hurt by what he regarded as shoddy treatment from the Bills' management.

"Other guys have gotten into fights or knocked management in order to get traded. I thought I'd played it straight, putting my wishes on the table—and I never thought that football would just say, 'Let him sit.'"

O.J. had some options, make no mistake. He was beginning what would be a lucrative acting career to match his well-paid and successful broadcasting career.

Yet, football was his first love, and he felt he owed a special allegiance to the sport that had taken him off Potrero Hill and made him a millionaire.

It looked as if the 1976/77 NFL season would be O.J.-free, but appearances are sometimes deceiving, and nobody counted on a last-minute appeal from a man that Simpson had come to admire and respect in his years in New York.

Buffalo Bills owner, Ralph Wilson, made an unprecedented move to regain his star running back. He flew to Los Angeles on Friday, September 10, just days after O.J. rejected the Bills "final" offer.

"As far as I am concerned," O.J. stated three days before Wilson's trip, "I am retired now."

There was always something of a father-and-son relationship between Simpson and Wilson.

In a 1976 interview with *Ebony* magazine, O.J. confessed that "businesswise, I always try to pattern myself after Ralph." Many in the broadcast world claim that Wilson coached Simpson in his negotiations with ABC Sports.

Wilson, a Detroit businessman who made his fortune in trucking and insurance, "was deeply hurt that O.J. wanted to leave the Bills," said a source close to both men during that season.

"It was like a son leaving a family, and it was intolerable to Wilson," that same source told a magazine in November, 1976.

Another factor in the Bills' owner's decision, one that was no doubt economic.

Wilson had experienced a taste of the Bills future without O.J. Simpson. Without O.J. on the field, Buffalo's attendance had dropped drastically, as much as forty percent.

One taste like that was enough for Wilson, who didn't want to lose his newly golden franchise.

Hat in hand, Wilson approached both O.J. and his wife Marguerite. They had briefly—though not legally—separated the year before and were now reconciled, and Wilson understood the pressures on family life that O.J. was facing.

"Ralph got to Los Angeles on a Friday," Simpson later told a reporter, "and he, my wife Marguerite, and I spent a good four hours talking at our house. His main point was that he had tried his best to make a trade for me but that it just hadn't worked out.

"[Wilson] said he felt it was the wrong time for me to retire from football, and that the Bills would like to have me back."

Wilson was reported as doing much of his talking to the stubborn Marguerite, who stood her ground. She preferred to raise her family in California, and that was that.

Money did not impress her—though the amounts being discussed certainly impressed O.J.

Marguerite maintained that she wanted O.J. around more than she wanted the money.

The football player's high-school sweetheart would not budge. She insisted on remaining in their Bel Air mansion, and she wanted O.J. there with her.

* * *

The Sunday following Wilson's eleventh-hour flight to Los Angeles was an eventful one. O.J. Simpson agreed to return to play for the Bills, and he would be there in time for the season opener.

Simpson was candid in December of that year, when he was interviewed by *Playboy*. "I can't say that money wasn't a big factor, but it wasn't the *major* factor."

Simpson made it clear to the press and to his teammates that his desire for a trade was not personal. O.J. just wanted to save his strained marriage.

For her part, Marguerite knew that O.J. was miserable about the situation, and more miserable about leaving football.

"I talked [to Wilson] a long time," explained O.J. in his *Playboy* interview. "He told us the kind of money the Bills were willing to pay, and when we had finished talking, I drove him back to his hotel.

"I still had no intention of playing for the Bills, but late that night, I changed my mind."

It was Marguerite who pushed him, Simpson admitted later.

"Marguerite said I had been a grouch for

about a week and that maybe my pride was getting in my way," he told *Playboy*.

"Pride can be a funny thing, because sometimes it can keep you from doing what you really want to do—and she thought that what I really wanted to do was play football.

"I was still being stubborn about it, but we finally decided that if Ralph cleared up some contractual things the next day, which was a Saturday, I'd leave for Buffalo on Sunday.

"Ralph cleared those things up at breakfast the next morning, so on Sunday I caught the first flight out to Buffalo."

His relationship with the Bills' fans remained rocky.

O.J. played the opening game, and judging from some of the boos he received that night, his reasons for holding out and his handling of the negotiations were taken as a ploy by Simpson to get more money out of the Bills management—which, in essence, he did.

After he agreed to return to the Bills he was given a three-year contract that was worth in excess of two and a half million dollars.

For his part, O.J. took the fans' negative reaction with a grain of salt.

"After I had carried the ball a few times, most of the boos turned to cheers, probably because the fans in Buffalo know that I'm there to play football and I don't give them anything but my very best."

Besides, "you gotta remember," O.J. told one interviewer, "Buffalo has the most vocal fans in the NFL, and they take the game very personally."

The complex negotiations and Ralph Wilson's personal intervention to get O.J. back to Buffalo initially, according to the superstar, helped his marriage to Marguerite.

Simpson told Pete Axehelm in 1976 that "the new contract will make life easier, or at least a lot more secure down the line.

"And the whole experience has also brought Marguerite and me a lot closer together."

Axehelm ended the 1976 article on an upbeat note.

"With his financial and marital cares behind him, O.J. should have an exciting season . . ."

Of course, as things turned out, O.J.'s marital problems were still not behind him.

His football career continued on track, though.

O.J. would go on to play two more seasons with the Bills, and he played them in top form. He also got out of his lucrative contract with ABC—for an even better offer from NBC.

NBC offered more money, but that wasn't the major reason for the star's departure from the American Broadcasting Company. The real reason he left was because NBC offered him a much more "creative" contract.

O.J., like Jim Brown, with whom he is often compared, was bitten by the acting bug. He made his first film, *The Klansman* which starred Richard Burton, and he was hooked. He liked hanging around on the set, drinking with Burton and his current wife, actress Elizabeth Taylor.

One day on the set, the conversation turned to food, and someone remarked that Chasen's restaurant had the best chili in the world. Without a beat, Elizabeth Taylor dispatched her Lear jet to fly a couple thousand miles and pick up some.

"That was some take-out," co-star Lee Marvin quipped.

This was the lifestyle O.J. wanted for himself.

NBC guaranteed that O.J. would not only work on various NBC sports programs, but he would also be featured in variety shows, comedy specials, and television movies—they also offered him a five-year contract.

He was playing his best, giving his best, to the Buffalo Bills, but by 1977 it was clear that this star player and record breaker was saddled with a mediocre team.

It was also clear to O.J. Simpson that he would probably never make it to the pinnacle of pro football, the Super Bowl.

In November, 1977, after running a paltry 557 yards, O.J. took another hit to his left knee—it turned out to be another season-ending injury.

He sat out his last year with the Bills on the bench. It was clear that the team management was not happy with him, nor was O.J. happy with them.

Even before the injury, O.J. began to grumble. The Bills had lost every one of their first three games of the 1977 season, and thirteen in a row the season before.

The Juice was mad.

After the fourth game of the season, where the New York Jets squeezed out a last-minute 24–19 win against the Buffalo Bills, Simpson gave an interview to New York's influential

African-American newspaper, the *Amsterdam News*.

"My ankle hurts," O.J. moaned, "my head hurts, and all I can think about is the game against Atlanta this Sunday.

"I'm really disappointed with all this losing, especially the way in which we're losing. We had a good week of practice and really had a lot of spirit coming into the game against the Jets.

"We really thought this was the week we were going to turn it around."

What followed was pretty bitter, reflecting Simpson's continued frustration.

"I can see that I'm not part of the Bills' future. They are rebuilding without me. I like work. I need it, but under this new philosophy, I just don't get enough work . . . I feel that the changes they are making are positive ones for the future, but that is no consideration to me.

"My future is now."

His bitterness was no doubt partly directed at himself. Simpson was forced to leave the game after a crunching tackle by Burgess Owens, who spoke of O.J. with contempt, mingled with sadness. Owens told reporters that he was playing a different man.

"He wasn't the same old O.J.," Owens insisted.

"He wasn't cutting back the way he usually does."

If fact, Owens had hurt O.J. once before, in a game between the Bills and the Jets, played on Halloween, 1976.

For the next several months after that first injury by Owens, Simpson experienced blurred vision and had trouble focusing—it wasn't until the following August that he was given a clean bill of health by specialists at the Wilmer Eye Institute of Johns Hopkins University Hospital in Baltimore. Doctors there declared his eyesight, "just one line below perfect."

Now, a year later, Owens had hit him again, and O.J. had to limp off the field.

"I guess his ankle was really bothering him," said fellow teammate Jerone Barkum, by way of an explanation.

Some of the Buffalo fans had another explanation.

O.J., they said, was getting old. He had just passed the big 3–0.

Things seemed to be winding down for O.J., but he was a man of many fancy moves—the "okey-doke," the "fake," the "sidestep,"—and he always managed to get up and go that extra inch.

In March of 1978, there was yet another twist in O.J.'s football career, which many fans and sports commentators thought was already over.

On March 24th, the Buffalo Bills traded O.J. to his hometown team, and he became a San Francisco 49er. He was a fourth round draft pick, and was traded by the Bills for five future 49ers' draft choices. O.J. had a new team, and a new lease on his professional life.

The running back made no effort to hide his jubilation over the completion of the trade in the early morning of the 24th, after hours of negotiations that lasted well into the night.

"Home at last. Great God almighty, I'm home at last," gushed a celebrating O.J. Simpson at the press conference held to announce the trade.

"O.J. is back," said the 49ers' general manager, Joe Thomas. Thomas had good reason to be jubilant as well—he didn't have to trade any of his current players to grab The Juice. Not only that, but Thomas didn't have to surrender any of his first round draft choices for that year—it was something of a sad commentary on how O.J.'s value had fallen since the two knee injuries and the two subsequent missed seasons.

At the time of the trade, Simpson himself thought that he could play two, perhaps even three more seasons of professional football. Simpson also indicated that he would make no more attempts to renegotiate his current contract—which paid him an impressive $700,000 a year. The amount, though shy of the deal he struck with Ralph Wilson, was pretty generous. After all, O.J. was no longer in his twenties, and he was damaged goods.

The trade came as no surprise. Simpson had again gone public with his dissatisfaction with the Bills, and he often stated to journalists and broadcasters that he was "frustrated" by the Bills performance overall. "Just once I'd like to play on a championship team," he told a reporter shortly after the trade.

O.J. hoped that the 49ers was that team.

For their part, the San Francisco team was trying to boost its reputation after several disappointing seasons—they needed an offensive spark, and they hoped O.J. would be the catalyst. The 49ers were also a team in a bit of financial trouble, and they hoped that O.J.'s popularity would bring in the fans.

Thomas, when asked about Simpson's ability to draw fans, remained noncommittal.

"O.J. will be most important on the field. If we get the job done there, the box office will take care of itself."

Thomas added that he had no doubts about O.J.'s appeal. Both Simpson and Thomas felt that the Bills would also benefit from the trade, since Chuck Knox was working hard to build that team back up through draft choices. And the Bills, due in part to O.J.'s injury early in the season, had a dismal three wins, and eleven losses the season before. But Knox was not altogether delighted with the deal that was made.

"The decision to trade a player like O.J. is a difficult one," Knox stated at the press conference to announce the trade.

"We had to weigh his undeniable short-range value to the club against the long-range prospect of building a challenging football team in Buffalo.

"He wanted to play on the West Coast, where he has many personal ties, and at this stage in his career, he deserves the opportunity to do so."

The trade allowed O.J. to play his final years of professional football in his home town, and on the West Coast, where his wife Marguerite always wanted him to be.

All things considered, the last season with the Bills and his first season with the San Francisco 49ers was both a sad and a happy time for O.J. Simpson. He left the Buffalo Bills with an impressive rushing and touchdown record, and he broke a few NFL records as well—though he never managed to beat "the big one," Jim Brown's career total. During his years with the Bills, O.J. Simpson's statistics read like this:

1969	181 attempts	697 yards	2 touchdowns
1970	120 attempts	488 yards	5 touchdowns
1971	183 attempts	742 yards	5 touchdowns
1972	292 attempts	1,251 yards	6 touchdowns
1973	332 attempts	2,003 yards	12 touchdowns
1974	270 attempts	1,125 yards	3 touchdowns
1975	329 attempts	1,817 yards	16 touchdowns
1976	290 attempts	1,503 yards	8 touchdowns
1977	126 attempts	557 yards	0 touchdowns

Simpson's single season (1973) rushing record still stands today.

The final two seasons of O.J.'s pro football career were somewhat anticlimactic. He never played for a championship team—the 49ers never even got close. But O.J. played hard, he played his heart out.

"The thing is, I want to leave the game like Jim Brown—who quit while he was still the best—and not like Johnny Unitas" Simpson told a reporter in 1975, when he was nearing thirty.

"Unitas was one of the greatest quarterbacks who ever played the game, but the young guys who saw him at the end of his career saw a guy who wasn't anywhere near the great player he'd been."

The same thing was true, O.J. felt, about one of his idols, Willy Mays. According to O.J., what people saw at the end of Mays career was, "almost a caricature of Mays.

"He was thick with age, his hat didn't fall off when he ran and he couldn't hit or run like he used to."

O.J. didn't want to end his football days like that.

He wanted to go out with style.

He began his second year with the San Francisco 49ers determined to try one last assault on Jim Brown's career rushing record of 12,312 yards. There were over 1,500 yards separating O.J. from Brown's record, but The Juice, despite his age—he was thirty-two, old for a football player, ancient for a running back—Simpson was motivated. He'd had ten outstanding seasons, and though the closest he ever got to a Super Bowl was the 1974 first-round loss for Buffalo in the playoffs, and though two seasons on the bench for injuries impacted on his goal of breaking Brown's record, O.J. Simpson was bound and determined to be a working member of the 49ers.

There were other records he wanted to shatter, as he told a reporter in 1979.

"Jim Brown's career record was an objective, sure, but I had two other objectives that I did not make either.

"I wanted to get 300 yards in a single game—nobody's ever done that—and I wanted to get six touchdowns in a game, like Gale Sayers did." He never pulled it off.

O.J. ended his thoughts on a philosophical note.

"I'll live without them," he told the interviewer.

The second year with the 49ers was marred by some controversy.

Dave Anderson did a feature article for the *New York Times* in which he stated that O.J. was doing just that—going out with style.

It was the end of his career, and 49ers

coach Bill Walsh had benched him for the last time.

"O.J. Simpson could have sulked or griped. After all, he was the celebrity who had announced he was closing out a glorious career, not the new coach. The public would have sympathized with him.

"But when Bill Walsh of the San Francisco 49ers benched him six weeks ago, Orenthal James Simpson showed his style . . . 'The coach,' he explained in his gentle manner, 'has to worry about the team for next season,' " Anderson wrote, clearly impressed with O.J.'s dignity and poise in the face of this blow to his pride.

Anderson recalled that that was O.J.'s way—to do things with both dignity and style. He wrote with admiration about the day that O.J. broke the rushing record in 1973, on a snowy day in Shea Stadium in New York.

"He upstaged his record after the game. In anticipation, a large room had been set aside for a mass news conference, but when O.J. arrived he had the ten other members of the Bills' offensive team with him.

"One by one, he introduced them.

" 'These are the cats who did the job all

year long,' he said. 'It's their record as much as mine.' "

When O.J. spent his last week with the 49ers, his teammates presented the sports legend with a solid gold money clip. In the clip was a fresh one dollar bill. "To get you started in your life after football," one of the 49ers joked.

His last days were sad ones, because many of the men he played with, and against, many of his fans and many of his coaches were quick to forget that he was one of the greatest running backs in the history of the game. He still had supporters, men like coach Don Shula, then with the Miami Dolphins, who when O.J. retired called him "the best pure runner of all time."

When O.J. ran 227 yards against the world champion Pittsburgh Steelers, and swept around, past and over the much-ballyhooed "Steel Curtain," Joe Green—Mean Joe—expressed his admiration.

"I didn't think anybody could do that to us, but O.J. did."

Of course, as Dave Anderson pointed out in his eulogy to Simpson's football career, O.J. did that to everybody. "First he was there, then he was gone," as Joe Green put it.

It was a feat he would repeat, fifteen years later, in Los Angeles.

Even after Jim Brown's phenomenal performance on the football field, O.J. Simpson's style was something special. No one had ever before seen his like.

He dodged, he weaved, he sidestepped, he jumped over and crawled under blockers, eluded tackles, made the score. O.J. ran circles around the obstacles set against him. And when those obstacles hit him the hardest, when he was hurt, when he was down— for a game, or for a season—he picked himself right back up and he was back.

It was the way he learned to live life. As a street kid he dodged the traps and pitfalls of youth in the ghetto. He faked his peers by dodging drugs, or faking it, as he would fake out a tackle closing in on him at the goal line.

O.J. was quick and smart and flashy on the football field, as he was in life. And nobody had ever seen his like.

"It was like a crazy, kung-fu Bruce Lee thing," said one fan of his Buffalo days.

"He'd appear in front of you—he'd look you in the eyes, and then he was gone," said Mean Joe Green.

"He was fast, he was loose, and you wonder how the hell he pulled it off," said an assistant coach for the 49ers.

But he was humble about his skills, about his drive and his power both on and off the playing field. His friends knew him as a workaholic, as a driven athlete, and they all recognized his competitive side.

"O.J. doesn't like to lose," Bills owner Ralph Wilson once said.

Simpson must have loved football as much as the game loved him. And why not. Running down the field, screaming fans on both sides of him urging him on with shouts of "Juice! Juice! Juice!" and "Run, O.J. Run!" Simpson himself probably thought that those days were past when he retired from the game that made his name a household word.

How could he have ever imagined that fifteen years after his last day on the playing field, he would be rushing down a highway in his beloved Los Angeles, the police—tackles in black-and-white chasing him—with his fans lining the highway, screaming in one voice.

"Run, O.J.! Run!"

"Now You See Him, Now You Don't" was the title of a *Sports Illustrated* piece written near the height of his gridiron career. This statement would also be true of Simpson years later, when O.J. was a much-sought after man—this time, though, he was a fugitive wanted on two counts of first-degree murder.

Seven

Because of planning, hard work and fore-sight—the kind of forward thinking O.J. dis-played when he held out for one more year in junior college so he could attend USC—Simpson had many ways to go after his grid-iron career came to a close.

He was still a popular broadcast personal-ity. He held a dozen lucrative promotional contracts for various products. And he was a movie star. His open, handsome face turned out to be very photogenic, and he never lacked for a part—in feature films, made for television movies, in guest spots on television series, and even on variety shows, though like most other Hollywood stars, his career had its high and lows.

O.J. Simpson's first taste of acting—aside from a tiny part in a forgettable film called "The Dream of Hamish Mose"—came when he guest starred in the CBS television series, *Medical Center* in 1969. This television show featured O.J. portraying a—surprise—college football star who was suffering from a disease and trying to hide that fact from his coach and his fans because he wanted to make the pros. It wasn't much of a stretch, and, as with most of the television at that time, the writing was abysmal.

Already, comparisons were being made to that other running back-turned-thespian, Jim Brown. In a *Sports Illustrated* feature in the July, 14, 1969 issue, Frank Deford wrote about Simpson's future in films and television.

"Acting is a serious future possibility. The natural comparison is with Jimmy Brown, who as a film hero has been generally dismissed as just another pretty face—but who has been hitting the box offices pretty hard. Simpson seems to be a better—loose and natural—rookie actor.

In that same article, Deford quoted an unnamed MGM studio executive, who stated, "The thing is, he never gets in his own way,"—an appraisal that seems particularly apt if the man never saw O.J. play football.

Al C. Ward, the producer of *Medical Center,* could not contain his gushing, and told Simpson "I just heard from the studio," Ward told the football legend, "and you're going to be a star! The dailies were marvelous; they're all raving about you down there.

"Now the only thing that scares me is that you'll become temperamental."

At the location shooting for this episode, done in Santa Monica in a cordoned off football field, children kept sneaking onto the set and badgering O.J. for autographs. Frank Deford described the scene:

" 'Hey, you O.J.?' one of the kids asked.

" 'Naw," O.J. said, 'that's O.J. over there'— pointing to Willie Brown.

" 'Right, O.J.? And that's Rap Brown'— pointing to Wes Grant. 'You know he's militant because he has a beard. Right, Rap?'

"The kids' delight showed on their faces. 'You gonna sign with Buffalo?' one of the asked.

" 'You think I ought to?' O.J. parried.

" 'How much you want?'

" 'How much do you think I'm worth?'

" 'I wouldn't give you 90 cents, Simpson," another kid said, and laughed.

" 'You play football?' Simpson asked him.

" 'Sure.'

" 'What position?'

" 'Quarterback," the boy said proudly.

" 'I figured you were a QB the way you talked all the time,' O.J. said."

Despite the fun on set, O.J. took the part very seriously, and often made suggestions that director William Graham actually accepted. His appearance on *Medical Center* was scheduled to be the fifth show to air in the series, but executives at the network were so impressed with his performance—and enamored of the ratings they hoped to pick up—that the O.J. episode was bumped up, to become the premiere episode of the series when it debuted in the fall.

Not all of his fans, nor many sports writers, were happy that The Juice had turned to Hollywood. Sports writers felt that it was a bad move for O.J. The general consensus among sports writers was, "why should the best running back in the NFL go to Hollywood to become a second-rate actor?"

And his admirers? Simpson himself related a story about the reaction of one of his fans in a 1979 article for *TV Guide*, a woman from his old neighborhood in South San Francisco.

"Miss James was this frail, grey-haired lady from my old Potrero Hills ghetto days.

"I didn't see her for ten years, but she prayed after me and sent me cards when I played for Buffalo. Then in 1978, when I was traded back out here, she came by to visit.

"We did fine until I mentioned my film

life, that I was making *Goldie and the Boxer* and *Detour.*

"Miss James was shocked. 'Moving pictures? Lord, O.J., please.' She started tearing up, dabbing her eyes with her lilac hanky.

"'Don't go to that Hollywood,' she begged me. 'You get in those moving pictures and first thing, they'll make you be a homosexual. O.J. please don't deny your football to be a homosexual.' "

O.J. pretty much disregarded Miss James' dire prediction, and went on to guest star in a number of forgettable and forgotten television series—*Cade's County, Owen Marshall, Counselor at Law,* etc. He even tried his hand at starring in his own series, and produced the pilot of the show, called *High Five.* In April of 1994, O.J. Simpson was still working on pilots—he starred in the first episode of a show about Navy SEALs, titled *The Frogmen.*

His feature film career started early, and really kicked in with his second theatrical feature, after the all-but-forgotten *The Dream of Hamish Mose,* in which he starred with some of the biggest names in show business.

In 1974 he was cast with Richard Burton, Lee Marvin, Cameron Mitchell, Lucianna Paluzzi, and Linda Evans in a turgid little "thriller" called *The Klansman*. It was a lack-luster feature film, directed by Terence Young, the veteran director of some of the finest James Bond blockbusters, including *Dr. No, From Russia, With Love* and *Thunderball*—which the Young made with Lucianna Paluzzi, an actress he cast in *The Klansman*.

Paluzzi was an interesting woman, and she made international headlines in the late 1960s by being one of the first women to get a legal divorce in Catholic Italy. O.J. played several scenes with this vivacious Italian beauty.

The film failed for a number of reasons. There wasn't enough physical action—director Young's strong suit—and the plot was so muddled, and so tawdry, that it was simply no fun to watch. Burton's performance was a little over-the-top, and the film's dark, gritty look turned off audiences.

Supposedly a serious film about race relations, the final edit eschewed any kind of real social message in favor of dull theatrics and cheap melodrama. Young's career was hurt by the failure of this film, and he did not direct again until the Japanese-American western, "Red Sun," which starred Charles Bronson as a gunfighter, and Toshiro Mifune as a samurai warrior on a mission along the Texas/Mexico border. Needless to say, this film, too was a flop.

But despite the bad reviews that came in about *The Klansman*, O.J.'s performance was given a polite nod—much the same way that Jim Brown's role as a vicious, condemned soldier sent on a suicide mission in *The Dirty Dozen* won him critical acclaim.

Of course, *The Dirty Dozen* was also a much better film.

During the filming of *The Klansman*, Academy Award-winning actor Lee Marvin, who had worked with Jim Brown in *The Dirty Dozen*, praised Simpson's performance. "Acting comes naturally to him," he stated. Marvin, an ex-Marine Corps drill instructor-turned actor with little formal theatrical training, recognized Simpson's natural acting ability—an ability that The Juice honed on the streets of San Francisco, where, in his own words, "I learned to talk my way out of bad situations while my brothers were hauled off to jail."

That same year, 1974, O.J. was the focus of a highly-rated ABC sports special entitled "Juice on the Loose," which was aired on the network in late December. O.J. was the subject of special broadcast because of his association with ABC Sports. But "Juice on the Loose," which also featured other ball-players from the Bills team, is a pretty impressive piece of documentary filmmaking. This documentary was directed by George Romero, who made his start in the motion picture industry by making television commercials for the Pittsburgh Brewery Company in his home town.

In 1968, Romero became famous—or infamous—when his first feature film, the *Night of the Living Dead* premiered. It so horrified some film goers that the esteemed Congresswoman, Margaret Chase Smith, wrote a scathing piece attacking the film, which was published in *Reader's Digest*. Today, *Night of the Living Dead* is considered a classic, and a print is enshrined in the New York Metropolitan Museum of Modern Art.

Romero had filmed several sports documentaries for the Steelers and several college teams, and his quick cutting and fast editing style was perfect for the physical action featured in these documentaries. Romero and financial partner Richard Rubinstein formed Laurel Tape and Film, Inc. in Pittsburgh and began to produce this series of sports specials for ABC television. "Juice on the Loose" was the tenth, and most successful, of these ventures.

In a feature article in *Filmmakers Newsletter*, April, 1975, called "The Selling of O.J. Simpson," the producer talked about the rewards and pitfalls of making sports documentaries, and a companion article in the same issue, written by Michael G. Gornick and S. William Hinzman, offered a behind the scenes look at the making of "Juice on the Loose."

"As we shot," the authors wrote, "we discovered the enthusiasm of O.J. and his teammates, as well as that of fans, old friends, people on the street, and children. In fact, our producer, Richard Rubinstein, stretched his budget to allow us to shoot an extra day in Buffalo to capture more of the atmosphere, so in all, we had four shooting days in Buffalo."

The documentary was pretty thorough, and even included a two-day shoot in O.J.'s old neighborhood of Potrero Hill. It included scenes of "O.J.'s high school to his parents' home on the south side; City College to . . . Eight thousand feet of exposed footage later, we bounded up the ramp at San Francisco Airport for our flight to Los Angeles and a reunion with 'The Juice.' "

During the course of the shooting, Gornick and Hinzman recall, the Simpsons gave the crew free reign of his home, "a freedom that amazed us all."

"O.J. and his wife, Marguerite, permitted us to store our equipment in the garage, conduct business and strategy meetings in the den, and dine around the pool.

"Graciously, the family lived in and around the confusion of crew members busily moving about the house shooting trophies, house interiors, exteriors, interviews with family and friends, and O.J. himself." Director Romero, Gornick and the film crew had trouble keeping up with Simpson's demanding pace. "As O.J. moved, we followed."

George Romero actually considered O.J. Simpson for the starring role in the sequel to *Night of the Living Dead*, made in 1978. Romero was an unconventional filmmaker, and actually cast a black man as the lead in the original *Night of the Living Dead*, something that wasn't done in 1968 unless the actor in question was Sidney Poitier. Unfortunately, shooting for *Dawn of the Dead* occurred in January and February in Monroeville, Pennsylvania (it was shot mostly in a shopping mall) and conflicted with Simpson's football season, and so the towering, 6'9" African-American actor Ken Foree got the part.

Simpson's second role in a feature film was opposite veteran superstars Paul Newman and Steve McQueen in the Irwin Allen production of *The Towering Inferno*. Producer Allen was famous for a couple of bargain-basement television series aired in the early 1960s. All of his shows had a science fiction premise, and were geared to the teen and pre-teen market. Not a creator of the caliber Gene Roddenberry, who produced the *Star Trek* television series, or Leslie Stevens, who wrote the screenplay for Alfred Hitchcock's *Psycho* and produced the legendary television series, *The Outer Limits,* Allen contented himself with making his first feature film hit, *Voyage to the Bottom of the Sea,* into a weekly television series that starred Richard Basehart and David Hedison—an actor famous for his role as *The Fly*. He also produced the television cult favorite, *Lost In Space,* and the forgettable *Land of the Giants.*

At the time it was filmed, Irwin Allen's production of *The Towering Inferno* was one of the most expensive films ever mounted, only eclipsed by the disastrous Taylor/Burton vehicle, *Cleopatra,* which bombed several years before. Twentieth-Century Fox got burned with *Cleopatra,* and other studios learned their lesson. Allen was permitted his "cast of thousands," his top-flight special effects, and his superstar leads—but only if, Warner Brothers executives insisted, another source of funding could be found to finance the tremendously expensive film.

Allen managed to get Fox involved, and *The Towering Inferno* became a joint partnership— the first time in history that two studios produced a single feature in cooperation. The story of a high-rise skyscraper that catches on fire on the eve of its dedication, trapping hundreds of high-society types on the roof, *The Towering Inferno* was the *Poseidon Adventure* of architecture. Audiences were treated to the sight of Robert Wagner burning to death, Fred Astaire as an aging gigolo, Jennifer Jones as his next mark, who plunges to her doom from the top floor, and O.J. Simpson playing Nordberg, the harried chief of building security.

While hundreds are dying upstairs, O.J.'s big scene is saving the life of Jennifer Jones' cat on a lower floor. His most poignant scene—or the unintentionally funniest, depending on one's point of view—is when O.J. presents the rescued cat to Astaire, who is mourning the loss of the meal-ticket Jennifer Jones.

O.J. next starred in a forgettable opus produced under the title *The Diamond Mercenaries,* but released in the United States—on the low-end "kung fu circuit" of drive-ins and third run theatres—as *Killer Force.* In this one, O.J. played a good-natured mercenary soldier in Africa who was intent, with his partners Peter Fonda (of *Easy Rider* fame), Christopher Lee (the venerable British actor most famous for his roles as Dracula and Dr. Frankenstein in a host of Hammer horror film produced in the 1960s), Hugh O'Brian and Maud Adams, to rob a South African diamond mine guarded by a sadistic head of security, played by Telly Savalas.

In many ways, this was Simpson's best role yet. It was certainly his most meaty. He was on-screen for much of the film, and he played the comedic foil to Christopher Lee's stiff, British straight man. Lee, portraying a sadistic killer who smiled every time he got to cut someone's throat with huge combat knife, was the perfect straight man. In one funny scene, O.J. is driving a Land Rover across the veldt in Africa, swerving and dodging obstacles in his path. Lee, disgusted with his performance, asks Simpson "Where did you get your drivers license?"

Without missing a beat, O, J, smiling,

quips, "Hey man, I won it in a crap game!"
Lee's response is a guttural snarl.

This film is also remembered by action/adventure fans for Hugh O'Brian's tender death scene, where he grunts, "Son of a bitch!" while bullets cut him down.

O.J.'s next opus was made after a two-year absence on the big screen. It was another internationally-produced disaster epic with a cast of thousands, called *The Cassandra Crossing*. This time he starred with Sophia Loren, Richard Harris, Ava Gardner, Burt Lancaster, Martin Sheen (Playing a gigolo—what '70s disaster film is complete without one?), and Lee Strasberg, the world-famous acting teacher who trained the likes of Marlon Brando, Robert DeNiro and Al Pacino. It was only Strasberg's second film role, after playing Jewish gangster Hyman Roth in the critically-acclaimed *The Godfather, Part II*. Strasberg, like Lee Marvin, expressed his surprise at O.J.'s "natural" acting ability.

The Cassandra Crossing shares elements with Stephen King's novel, *The Stand*: A government laboratory is robbed, but one of the thieves, an industrial spy, is doused with a dangerous biological weapon—a disease-bearing liquid that first gives its victims flu-like symptoms, and then kills them. The thief escapes from the U.S. military facility, located in Europe (Well, this *was* internationally-produced and financed) and hides aboard a passenger train, where he begins to infect the passengers.

Harris, a noted biologist and physician, is luckily aboard. So is his ex-wife, played by Sophia Loren, and through the course of the film they rekindle their romance. Burt Lancaster, playing another psychotic American general in the tradition of his role in *Seven Days In May*, orders the train sealed. In an effective and eerie sequence, the train is sidelined and surrounded by soldiers wearing head-to-toe white biological weapon-proof suits. When he sees them pushing passengers around and sealing everyone in the train, Strasberg, who plays a concentration camp survivor, has an ugly flashback to Nazi Germany. "Not again," he cries in alarm.

While Richard Harris is trying to find a way to stop an epidemic and cure the disease, Burt Lancaster orders the train sidelined down an old, abandoned railway that ends at a rickety, unused railroad bridge that is ready to collapse—all the better to make it look like a train wreck and cover the whole thing up.

Needless to say, the symbolism here is

pretty heavy-handed, but the climactic train wreck is pretty impressive.

O.J. actually had to do some research for his role in *The Cassandra Crossing*, as he told his *Playboy* interviewer in 1976.

"The role I play in *The Cassandra Crossing* was written for James Coburn, but when he got tied up in another movie, they got me. I play a priest in it."

Judging from what O.J. told *Playboy*, his preparation for the role actually thrilled Marguerite.

"I sort of surprised my wife for the last two months before I went to Rome to make the film by going to church with her every Sunday," he explained in his interview. "She's Catholic. And after church, I would speak to some of the priests in San Francisco who used to work with the baseball teams that I was on . . .

"I made it a point to look them up, just to be around them, to pick up maybe a few of their mannerisms, how they said things and how they kind of carried themselves.

"I watched them and I thought, if I were a priest, how would I act? That's pretty much my approach to all the roles I've gotten into; it's worked for me."

O.J. especially liked working with Richard

Harris and Sophia Loren, who made him feel at ease on a relaxed set. While with Marvin, Burton and the visiting Elizabeth Taylor on the Oroville, California location shoot for *The Klansman*, things were a bit more raucous.

O.J., it turned out, was the only actor on set of *The Klansman* who wasn't drunk most of the time.

"Oh, there was some vodka *absorbed*, Jack. Like cases and cases of it." Simpson later told an interviewer. O.J. also learned one trick of the acting trade you don't get studying under Lee Strasberg.

"I learned that in the acting industry, the heavy drinkers all go for vodka, because it doesn't smell."

O.J. spoke candidly about the antics that went on while filming *The Klansman*. Apparently, Richard Burton would get drunk and then he "would start ramblin' on in that booming voice of his, maybe recitin' from *Camelot* or something, just to get your attention."

Lee Marvin and the rest of the cast were pretty "laid back," and played a game they invented. In his 1976 *Playboy* interview, Simpson recalled that while Burton sang, the rest of the cast would stage a little contest in which they would all try to ignore his rambunctious antics.

"We'd play the game in which we'd all try to ignore him, but we couldn't."

Simpson told *Playboy* that he did admire one quality possessed by the gifted Welsh actor. "I've never seen a cat, tipsy or not, who could charm a lady more than Richard could."

The sets of *Killer Force* and *The Cassandra Crossing* were tame by comparison.

When he arrived in Rome to shoot *The Cassandra Crossing*, O.J. heard somebody yelling "Juice! Juice!" and then launch into a play-by-play description of one of his big games.

"I looked around and it was Richard Harris," O.J. told *Playboy*. "He was describing one of the big plays of the past season, so I knew he was a fan. He came up and made me feel at ease."

Sophia Loren made a big impression on Simpson. So much so that he discussed her in his interviews with *Playboy* and Andy Warhol's *Interview*. He was, like many men who have seen this remarkable woman in person, dumbfounded by her beauty. She actually made him feel a little shy and awkward. But she soon put him at ease.

"Sophia Loren, the first day I was on the set, noticed me watching her when she had a little break," he told *Playboy*. "She said, 'Come over and sit down,'" and she started helping me with a little Italian. Later she became my gin partner. Whenever we were on the set, we were playing gin.

"She's a great poker player, too," Simpson added in *Interview*.

In 1976, a group of women called Man Watchers, Inc. polled its 2,000 or so members in the United States, Great Britain, Australia and Canada and came up with the ten "most watchable" men in the world.

O.J. Simpson topped the list.

He beat out such 1970s notables as Kris Kristofferson, Chevy Chase, John Davidson, Nick Nolte, James Garner, Henry Winkler, David Hartman, former co-star Richard Harris, and Don Meredith.

Suzy Mallery, the president of Man Watchers, Inc, said that Simpson's "strong, good features and a well-built body" won him the title.

O.J.'s next dramatic project was a much more impressive production, the most-watched television mini-series in history. It was the 1977 mini-series based on the book *Roots* by Alex Hailey. The mini-series "Roots" was a colossal affair, a true milestone in television history. While it, too, featured a cast of thousands, unlike the other dramatic projects O.J. had worked on in the past, it was a huge cast of African-Americans. This time around, O.J. wasn't—in the jargon of the time—"the token Negro," and he didn't play a security guard as he did in *The Towering Inferno*. Also, unlike O.J.'s first film, *The Klansman*, this project didn't *pretend* to be about race relations.

With "Roots," Simpson was part of an impressive cast of African-American thespians who came into their own as a result of the emotional power and compelling drama of this monumental mini-series. Unfortunately for O.J., his part was a small one. But how could it be otherwise, for the cast was as large as it was impressive.

Along with LeVar Burton, now familiar to television viewers as Commander Jordie La-Forge on *Star Trek: The Next Generation,* but then a relatively unknown actor, Ben Vereen, Cicely Tyson and host of other actors and actresses, Simpson portrayed the African-American experience with poignancy and intelligence.

O.J. had to confront his ethnic heritage early in life, as all African-Americans must. The ghetto experience did not seem to traumatize him as it would other blacks of his and subsequent generations, probably because he had a loving and supportive home life. As he matured, he also possessed a focus as well as a drive and ambition to use his talents to the fullest. But, like every African-American, sooner or later O.J. would run into a wall of prejudice.

He was pretty good at handling the bigotry of others, and he was quick to point out that those negative experiences were not limited to the American South. As his fame grew, he gained more respect from those around him, but the specter of racism would still occasionally raise its ugly head. In an insightful interview, Simpson elaborated on his strategy for dealing with the bigots who approached him, usually in public places.

"I've been in places in the South—and also in the North—where some dude started making race remarks. But when the loudmouths say those kinds of things, I just make 'em disappear; to me, they're not even there.

"Of course, you can only take it so far and they you gotta let a guy know he's out of line . . . I ignore them until they try to pull me over to where they are.

"That's when Hertz comes in."

Referring to his most famous commercial ad campaign, and his position as the official spokesperson for Hertz for over a decade, O.J. elaborated.

"I give 'em a hard little jab in the chest

and say, 'Hertz, *don't* it? Not Avis—Hertz.' Politely, you let 'em know they're startin' to walk on thin ice."

In 1977, O.J. also starred in a critically-acclaimed made-for-television movie called "A Killing Affair." This film was considered groundbreaking at the time, because O.J. was cast as the romantic interest opposite Elizabeth Montgomery. Montgomery, something of an "America's sweetheart" icon like Mary Tyler Moore, because of her long-running and still syndicated television series, "Bewitched," in which she played Samantha the witch, here played a torrid woman lusting after her sexy African-American cop partner.

Interracial romance was still considered somewhat taboo on television at that time, but the medium had come a long way since Southern stations refused to air an episode of *Star Trek* in which William Shatner kisses Nichelle Nichols, in the mid-1960s.

O.J.'s next film project was another sympathetic role, and a larger part than he had in "Roots."

Capricorn One was another government-paranoia film like *The Cassandra Crossing*. He wasn't in the film because he had a fondness for such parts, nor did he share the screenwriter's politics. He was in the film because

O.J. Simpson accepting the 1968 Heisman Trophy during his senior year at the University of Southern California. (*AP/Wide World Photos*)

O.J. Simpson in his Buffalo Bills uniform with his own
number: 32.   (*Globe Photos, Inc.*)

O.J. Simpson set a new NFL single-season rushing record of 2,003 yards when the Bills played the New York Jets in December 1973. (*AP/Wide World Photos*)

O.J.'s last game. He was playing for the San Francisco 49ers when he announced his retirement on December 9, 1979 at pre-game ceremonies, then played against the Tampa Bay Buccaneers.
(*AP/Wide World Photos/Paul Sakuma*)

O.J. and his high school sweetheart, Marguerite Whitley,
who became his first wife. They divorced in 1979.
(*Nate Cutler/Globe Photos, Inc.*)

One of the first photographs of O.J. and his new flame, Nicole Brown, at a 1980 party in Beverly Hills. (*AP/World Wide Photos*)

O.J. and Nicole Brown, after she became his second wife. (*Dominguez/Globe Photos, Inc.*)

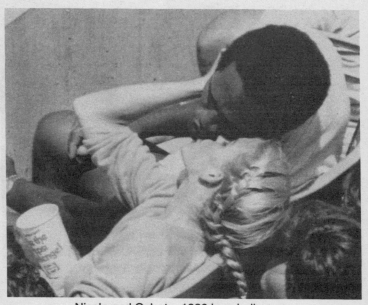

Nicole and O.J. at a 1980 baseball game. (*AP/Wide World Photos*)

Shortly before the tragedy, O.J. made a pilot for a
projected TV series, "Frogmen." To prepare for the action
series, he trained with a former Navy SEAL.
(*Globe Photos, Inc.*)

One of O.J.'s most important films was "Towering Inferno" in which he starred with Paul Newman and Jennifer Jones. (*Orlando/Globe Photos, Inc.*)

O.J. has always given back to the community. Here he is with Marc Buoniconti and Brooke Shields at a benefit for those with spinal injuries.
(*John Barrett/Globe Photos, Inc.*)

O.J. hands out gifts to the needy for the 5th Annual
Madison Avenue Christmas for Children Fund in 1991.
(*John Barrett/Globe Photos, Inc.*)

O.J. always made time for his family. Pictured here:
daughter Arnell by his first marriage.
(*Michael Ferguson/Globe Photos, Inc.*)

O.J. with his children by Nicole: daughter Sydney and son Justin. (*Castilla/Globe Photos, Inc.*)

1991 driver's license photo of the former Homecoming Queen of Dana Hills High School, Nicole Brown Simpson. (*AP/Wide World Photos*)

Police tape surrounds the Brentwood townhouse where Nicole Brown Simpson was found murdered, shortly after midnight, on Sunday, June 12, 1994. (*AP/Wide World Photos/Eric Draper*)

The curious gather in front of the townhouse where
Nicole and her companion were found murdered. Their
blood is still on the tiled walkway.
(*AP/Wide World Photos/Robert Hanashiro*)

Grim-faced O.J. and his attorney, Howard Weitzman, are besieged by media as they leave police headquarters in downtown Los Angeles on Monday, June 13, after O.J. was questioned for four hours about the murders of his ex-wife and her companion.
(*AP/Wide World Photos/Michael Caulfield*)

Howard Weitzman, O.J.'s attorney, withdrew from the case on Wednesday, June 15, citing personal commitments. (*AP/Wide World Photos/Michael Caulfield*)

Robert Shapiro, who became O.J.'s new lawyer that Wednesday. (*AP/Wide World Photos/Mark T. Terrill*)

An undated family photograph of Ronald Goldman,
found murdered with Nicole Brown Simpson.
(*AP/Wide World Photos*)

Fred Goldman, center, father of the late Ronald
Goldman, is flanked by daughter Kim, left and wife Patti,
as he addresses the media outside the family's Agoura
Hills, California, home on Wednesday, June 15, 1994.
(*AP/Wide World Photos/Tara Farrell*)

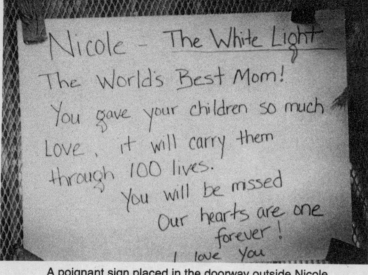

A poignant sign placed in the doorway outside Nicole Brown Simpson's condominium two days after her body was found there. *(AP/Wide World Photos/Nick Ut)*

Another moving sign, this one placed outside the gates
of O.J.'s mansion, on the same day.
(*AP/Wide World Photos/Michael Caulfield*)

Yet another sign, this one posted at the West Los Angeles Police Station amid false reports that O.J. had surrendered himself to police there.
(*AP/Wide World Photos/Eric Draper*)

A media circus set up outside O.J.'s mansion, clogging
the streets outside.
(*AP/Wide World Photos/Michael Caulfield*)

An unidentified visitor speaks into the intercom outside
O.J.'s gates. In spite of the throngs of media parked
there, the football great managed to slip past them to
attend a memorial service for his slain ex-wife at a
Laguna Hills mortuary.
(*AP/Wide World Photos/Michael Caulfield*)

that kind of thing was about the only adventure fare being made in those days—this was the 1970s.

This time, though, the evil conspiracy wasn't hatched by the U.S. military—convenient villains since the war in Vietnam—this diabolical scheme was hatched by NASA! O.J. played an astronaut on an ill-fated mission to Mars. It seems that NASA bureaucrat Hal Holbrook figured out that the mission was headed for disaster, so to save funding for the space program, he pulls the three astronauts out of the capsule and *stages* the Mars landing instead, on a Hollywood backlot. The fake landing is broadcast on live television.

The stalwart astronauts, O.J., Sam Waterston, and James Brolin, tumble onto the fact that they are supposed to die "when their capsule explodes in space" so the secret can never be revealed—a hell of a way to save your funding! The astronauts try to escape, and O.J. and Waterston get captured by government lackeys. Brolin manages to survive and is rescued by crusading reporter Elliott Gould—remember, this was after Watergate—who exposes the plan of the wicked Holbrook, and probably shuts down the space program for good!

O.J. was particularly praised for his performance in this film, and his role was a heroic and pivotal one. Despite the absurd premise of the film, overall, it was pretty effective, won critical acclaim, and did big box office. Up to that time, with the exception of the role he played in "Roots," this was the best part Simpson ever had, and one of his finest performances as an actor.

Eight

Sadly, his successful role in the box office smash *Capricorn One* came at a time in O.J.'s life when he couldn't really enjoy it. In February, 1977, the year that *Capricorn One* began filming, *Parents Magazine* did a feature article on the seemingly idyllic domestic life the Simpson family enjoyed. The article appeared in the middle of his last season with Buffalo, and the Simpsons spoke candidly about O.J.'s and Marguerite's difficulty dealing with the long separations during football season and when the superstar was working on location.

They also spoke honestly about the impact his career had on their two children, their daughter Arnelle, who was born December 4, 1968, and their son, Jason, who was born on April 20, 1970.

The article, written by Patricia Baum, also rehashed O.J.'s problems when the Bills couldn't find a way to trade him to a West Coast team and Ralph Wilson's eleventh-hour trip to convince the reluctant athlete to return for another season.

"So again this year," Ms. Baum wrote, "with Marguerite's reluctant agreement, O.J. ended up in Buffalo. Marguerite came to visit on weekends, but O.J. was able to see his children only twice before Christmas."

Ms. Baum went on to write about O.J.'s sensitivity to his wife's concerns, and of his forced absence—especially due to the fact that his father had left his mother when he was just four years old. O.J. understood what missing a father was like, and for one of the first times in his life, he spoke candidly about his father in print.

"Except for holidays, when I was growing up I rarely saw my father. I resented his absence, especially when I became a teenager, and was trying to find out who I was. I really needed a man around then for guidance.

"I get along with my father now, but it's taken years for me to come to terms with my feelings. Of course, my children aren't adolescents yet, but I'm already concerned that I'm not with them enough for my opinions to carry weight, or for me to follow through on my ideas."

In the article, O.J. expressed his "ideas" about child-raising, ideas that centered mainly on finding just the right balance between healthy freedom and necessary restrictions.

"I don't want my children gone all day . . . But I do want them to test themselves. I want to keep them safe without being overprotective and suppressive."

His philosophy sprang, he said, from his own upbringing on Potrero Hill. He was allowed to go out and play ball in the afternoons after school and on weekends, but he was still expected by his mother to do his chores and his homework.

O.J. talked about the Simpson family routines—about how Arnelle and Jason were expected to keep their rooms clean and neat, and their role in keeping the house clean. O.J. confessed that he was not a strict disciplinarian, but he had a plan to deal with "serious misbehavior."

First, he told *Parents Magazine*, he "gives a warning.

"If they fail to heed that, he'll follow with a spanking."

Modern family therapists are probably cringing as they read this, but O.J. believed that he was correct in this regard.

"Talking to them endlessly gets us nowhere," he stated, "whereas, if I spank them, they are calm and repentant afterward. And they know I still love them even though they had to be punished." Spankings, according to Marguerite, were very rare in the Simpson home. Of course, she was the parent with almost total responsibility for the children, as O.J. was seldom home.

Simpson, too, worried about his own fame, and how it would impact on his children. He had made several television commercials with his son Jason, but the superstar was concerned that about his son's privacy. "I want him to have privacy and time to himself, to learn who he is before he acquires a public image."

It was a picture of domestic bliss that was painted with words—not without problems—but as loving, supportive, and solid and secure.

It was not a portrait of a family that was headed for tragedy and divorce. Within a few months of the appearance of this article, Marguerite had a third child, a daughter, named Aaren. The birth of a third child seemed to signal their friends and acquaintances that the rocky times were over. They bought a new house, this time in the Brentwood section of Los Angeles—of course, for Marguerite's and the children's sake, it had a full-sized swimming pool.

Those who knew them both were doubly relieved when The Juice was traded to the 49ers—it looked as Marguerite was finally getting what she wanted, her man home year-round.

Another article, published in *Sports Illustrated* back in 1973, gives a very similar image of the couple. In that article, Marguerite calls her husband, "a typical Cancer.

"He's a homebody. He wants security. He likes a roof over his head and three meals a day . . ."

Was she talking about O.J. Simpson? O.J., the football star, was a man who was never home for more than a month at a time, and never during football season. He slept in hotels, or in a lonely apartment he had in Buffalo. Both these articles speak of a domesticated husband and father, yet Marguerite—and later Nicole Brown—would often complain that O.J. did not take an active part, nor show much interest, in his children or his home.

It was only a matter of time before the pictures painted in these two articles would clash with reality.

By September of 1978, Marguerite and O.J. were separated—this time legally. By the end of March, 1979, O.J. filed for a divorce. Marguerite gained custody of the children, and after some lengthy deliberations, it was eventually decided that O.J. would keep what he called his "dream house" in Brentwood. But that decision came later.

In California, it's "the fifty-fifty" split, according to divorce attorney Harry Fain, who represented Marguerite in the somewhat bitter divorce—which was characterized at the time as "friendly" by attorney Fain, even though both parties disagreed about the size and value of the community property to be divided.

When Fain was questioned about the reasons for the split, he was asked point blank by a reporter for *People* if the cause was O.J.'s womanizing. Fain's reply was guarded.

"Frankly, we haven't gone into the reasons for the divorce," he said, "but I would say she knew or sensed it."

She probably more than sensed it, for about this time, the name of a certain blond teenaged-beauty queen from Laguna Beach began to be mentioned in connection with O.J. According to the *New York Post*, dated April 19, 1979, "The Juice" was "still keeping company with his girlfriend Nicole Brown."

O.J. was less than candid about the split.

He blamed the divorce on "the price of fame . . .

"(It) was our biggest problem," he said. "My wife is a private person, yet we can't walk down the street without causing a commotion."

The irony was that, due to present and past injuries, O.J.'s football career was effectively over—and so was his marriage.

TRAGEDY STRIKES O.J.
AND MARGUERITE

This continued to be a difficult period in O.J. Simpson's personal life. In March of that year, O.J.'s former manager, Chuck Barnes, drowned in a boating accident off the California coast. In April, the same month he filed for a divorce, O.J.'s personal friend and adviser Carroll Rosenbloom, the owner of the Los Angeles Rams, perished in the Florida surf. Simpson told Jack Hicks, a feature writer for *TV Guide*, that when he got a call that his cousin's child had drowned, he thought "my God, when will this stop?

"I called my wife and begged her to give the kids swimming lessons and to watch them around the pool."

Four and a half months later, an even more terrible tragedy struck O.J. and his now ex-wife. On August 18 of that same year, a hot summer afternoon in Southern California, Aaren Simpson, the twenty-three-month-old daughter of Marguerite and O.J., somehow escaped her playpen and wandered down to the swimming pool. She was discovered missing a few minutes later, and a frantic search was on. She was located only minutes after that, facedown in the pool. Aaren Simpson lingered in a coma at UCLA Medical Center for a week before she died, one week shy of her second birthday.

When the divorce settlement was finalized, it was O.J. who got the Brentwood estate, full-size swimming pool and all. The house would remain O.J.'s primary residence until June 17, 1994.

After his divorce, and the tragic loss of his youngest child, O.J.'s focus on his movie career began to slip. He chose parts that were no better than walk-ons, or cardboard characters with few lines and little depth. There was only one role in this period that interested him, and it was a part he had been grooming himself for, and researching, for a period of three years.

O.J. Simpson had focused on another goal.

He wanted to play Coalhouse Walker, Jr. in the motion picture adaptation of E.L. Doctorow's epic novel, *Ragtime*. He had read the novel back in 1976, and in December of that year, when *Playboy* interviewed him, he was re-reading Doctorow's opus in preparation for an audition.

He was so determined to play the part that he was ready, then and there, to quit football for good—at the height of his gridiron career—to star in the Dino De Laurentiis production if it was scheduled to shoot in the fall.

Like Jim Brown, who cut short his pro football career to act in films like 1968's *Dark of the Sun*, with Rod Taylor, O.J. was ready to throw aside his athletic career for a shot at a star on Hollywood's Walk of Fame. He saw the character of Coalhouse Walker, Jr. as an instant ticket to stardom.

In his 1976 *Playboy* interview, O.J. explained: "There are certain parts that can build a movie career very quickly—and I think that Coalhouse Walker is one of those parts. They don't come around that often, either."

In January, 1976, Simpson reiterated his interest in the role of Walker to Red Smith, sports columnist for *The New York Times*. He told Smith that he even went so far as to mail a photograph of himself, wearing a beard, to Robert Altman, who was then set to direct the adaptation.

"That Coalhouse Walker part, I'm sure I could play him. I don't look like him but I've got his attitude," The Juice told Smith.

Unfortunately for O.J.'s acting career, the film version of *Ragtime* was delayed a couple of times, and Simpson went on to play for the Bills in the 1977 season. When the film *was* eventually produced, in 1981, Milos Forman directed, and Harold E. Rollins, Jr. got the role O.J. had coveted for years—but perhaps O.J. was lucky. Few thought the film was worthy of the novel, and it was critically panned.

Only Jimmy Cagney, in his final film role, got any sort of recognition. Harold E. Rollins didn't become a superstar, or even a household name, until he co-starred on television with Carroll O'Connor years later. *Ragtime*, the movie, was a box office dud.

In 1979 O.J. played opposite Sophia Loren, his co-star in *The Cassandra Crossing*, and James Coburn in the turkey, *Firepower*. He followed that with *Hambone and Hillie*, a sweet little film starring silent-movie actress Lillian Gish as an old woman who makes a three-thousand mile trek to find her lost dog. It was family fare, and O.J. was to turn out more of the same—both as a producer and as a star.

In 1978, O.J. formed Orenthal Productions. Originally the company was to be a partnership, but some of the key players backed out at the last minute. O.J. was undeterred and created the company himself. He produced a number of shows, including the comedy pilot *High Five*, the adventure film *Detour to Terror*, and probably the most successful of his production ventures, a film-for-television entitled "Goldie and the Boxer."

After the success of the inspirational *Rocky*, but before the gritty and gloomy *Raging Bull*, boxing films were in. Sylvester Stallone went on to make several sequels to his Oscar-winning boxing opus; Jon Voight remade *The Champ*, and Tom Berenger starred in the depressing *Flesh and Blood*, based on a novel by Pete Hamill.

O.J. Simpson decided to enter the fray with "Goldie and the Boxer." This made for television movie could be described as "Shirley Temple meets Sugar Ray Leonard." The film, set in 1946, tells the story of Joe Gallagher, a returning veteran of the Second World War heading for his home in Louisiana.

Joe is robbed by thugs and ends up broke

and battered in a small Pennsylvania town. There he is befriended by little Goldie, a cute moppet with blond curly hair and an adorable smile. Goldie's dad is a run-down boxer, and Joe joins his training camp as a sparring partner.

Dad dies suddenly, and Joe takes his place on the fight circuit with little Goldie as his manager. Things get pretty predictable from there, and it all winds up with a happy ending. Goldie was played with charm by Melissa Michaelson, and Phil Silvers was delightful as a dizzy, manic trainer. But it was O.J.'s performance as Joe that won the most applause. John J. O'Connor, in his review of the show in *The New York Times*, praised Simpson's performance.

"In addition to being good-looking, he has an appealingly warm and sincere personality which, under the direction of David Miller, is marketed effectively in the film."

"Goldie and the Boxer" aired on NBC, and garnered enough praise and Nielsen Ratings to merit a less impressive sequel, also produced by Orenthal Productions, called "Goldie and the Boxer Go to Hollywood."

O.J. then went on to play a hard-boiled San Francisco detective in another Orenthal production, this one with the unlikely title

"Cocaine and Blue Eyes." This film, which aired on New Year's Eve, had a holiday flair with tough-guy lines like "Last night's confetti is this morning's soggy trash." The film is set on a wet and miserable New Year's Day.

Everything about private eye Mike Brennen's life is miserable—from the soulful trumpet that is a constant source of irritation on the music track, to the way he gets knocked around in dark alleys, rain-swept streets, and hard-boiled women. O.J. played Brennen with a kind of campy, but undeniable charm, though critic John J. O'Connor was only mildly impressed.

Said O'Connor, "Mr. Simpson's acting abilities are minimal.

"He is attractive, he moves gracefully, and he can read a line without being laughable.

"He is, in brief, an acceptable presence, quite capable of hawking car rentals or getting through a rather silly television movie."

Best line: After O.J. is hit over the head in a dark alley, he quips, in traditional hard-boiled style, "I was kissing concrete instead of women."

Orenthal Productions also announced, in 1985, the production of *Heart and Soul*, the first African-American soap opera. Billed as a "soap opera with soul," it was scheduled to air in early February, 1986. The show was conceived as a daily show set against the backdrop of the music industry. Orenthal Productions forged a partnership with Columbia Pictures Television to make *Heart and Soul,* and Black Entertainment Television president Bob Johnson was brought aboard to handle day-to-day production and distribution. The project was dumped when Columbia backed out six months later, the series folded before an episode was aired.

Though he remained a player in Hollywood, starring in low-budget fare like *C.I.A.: Code Name Alexa,* and making occasional guest appearances, he didn't have much real Hollywood success again until the 1980's, when he played an inept police detective in the hugely successful *Naked Gun* films. *Naked Gun: From the Files of the Police Squad* featured Leslie Nielsen as Detective Frank Drebin, who also revitalized his sagging career with these lucrative films.

The first film, in the *Naked Gun* series was a 1988 big-screen rehash of the failed television series from the 1982 television season called *Police Squad,* conceived as a spoof of the Quinn Martin productions of the 1960s and '70s, most notably the Karl Malden/Michael Douglas show, *The Streets of San Fran-*

cisco. The film, like the series, was produced by the creative team of Jim Abrams, David Zucker and Jerry Zucker, who scored big box office success with their own brand of silliness when they filmed a low budget spoof of *Airport,* called *Airplane!* in 1980. This creative team continued their success with *Top Secret!,* a spoof of spy films, war pictures, and Elvis Presley films made in 1984.

Naked Gun: From the Files of the Police Squad showcased O.J.'s comedic abilities. He played an accident-prone police detective who gets dragged by a car, shot into the air, rolled down a flight of steps in a wheelchair, and hit with various heavy, blunt objects. His slapstick pratfalls sent audiences into hysterics, and he was cast in the equally-successful 1991 sequel, *Naked Gun 2 1/2: The Smell of Fear.*

He got hurt a lot in that one, too.

It looked as if O.J. Simpson was due for a resurgence in popularity. In addition to the third *Naked Gun* film, he was working on the pilot for an adventure series called *The Frogmen,* based on the exploits of the famed special forces group, the Navy SEALs (Sea, Air, Land) combat specialists. He was even trained by retired Navy SEALs in preparation for this role.

His Hollywood comeback, however, was cut tragically short by the events of June, 1994.

Nine

O.J. Simpson was probably the greatest all-around runningback in the history of football. He was a consummate athlete on the playing field, and a worthy competitor. He won the admiration of his teammates, the men he played against, and millions of Americans, who love and respect this living legend to this day.

There was probably only one thing that O.J. could do as well as play football, and it wasn't acting.

Orenthal James Simpson could make money. As a teenager he fished off Pier 90 and sold his catch for pocket money, scalped tickets, planned parties and charged admission. When these marginally honest endeavors failed, he stole pies from the bakery, staged fights in liquor stores with his buddies to distract the guy at the register long enough to grab a few bottles, or simply took what he wanted from somebody smaller and less aggressive than he was, financially, O.J. always managed to come out on top.

From the "free market" economy of the ghetto, he segued easily into the adult world of capitalism. Early on, O.J. knew that you had to have money to make money—he learned that simple economic fact scalping tickets, because you had to have tickets to scalp. "The Juice" knew you needed "juice"—money—and he knew that a poor urban kid who was not an academic whiz had little chance to rise much past the mailroom, or, in our current "service economy," the grill at Mickey D's.

So how does a poor black kid do it?

There are a hundred ways, if your not squeamish, if you're willing to go south of the law—your options are more limited if you have a conscience.

O.J. was something of a punk—but he *had* a conscience.

O.J. chose sports. Either he had the wisdom, early in life, to focus his energies to what he must have considered his last, best hope, or he simply possessed a genuine, God-given gift for the sport of football. Probably it was both. O.J. didn't just wish, he *did*. He was a man of action, compelled to run through the business world the way he ran through defensive linemen, turning, twisting, struggling for that extra inch.

And as with football, O.J. had well-honed instincts. He could smell a good business deal the same way he could spot the crack's in an opponent's defensive. He could exploit them both. And it wasn't even work—he *loved* it. He wanted fame the way a virgin wants a bride, and he courted it like an impatient suitor. It was always go, go, go. Push harder, do more, go that extra inch, that extra mile.

Pro football and the acclaim that goes with it would have been enough for many men. The money would have been enough for most. It was not enough for O.J.

The telling phrase, "Don't ever say enough to me," has been attributed to the Marquis de Sade.

That phrase seemed to be O.J. Simpson's credo.

O.J. THE ENTREPRENEUR

Pro football, broadcasting, commercial endorsements, movie acting—each of these fields of endeavors pay handsomely. If the "commodity" in question is on top of any one of these professions, the financial rewards are astronomical.

O.J. Simpson, for a time, was on top of them all.

O.J. the entrepreneur.

"Here comes O.J. Simpson," Billy Rowe once wrote in a 1977 column in the *Amsterdam News*.

"The running star of the Buffalo Bills with talents oozing out of every pore taking the lead with more than a million bucks a year.

"He earns this through his $400,000 salary when he wears cleats, and through maybe a dozen endorsements and promotions . . .

"Now he's getting starring roles in films and TV, and has landed a contract as a sports commentator with NBC and owns his own production company.

"Yep, 'The Juice' has oozed past the one mission dollar annual class. He's rated for credibility, persuasiveness, sales effectiveness and merchandisability.

"And it's a talent that caused *Advertising Age* to elect him Star Presenter of the Year, succeeding Karl Malden, last year's Oscar winner as an advertising celebrity performer."

Much of O.J. "credibility" was a result of his visibility. In the late 1970's, when Simpson was at his peak earning years, his face was everywhere. He was one of the most recognized men in America.

In a 1976 *Ladies Home Journal* public opinion poll, conducted among American school children in the fifth through the twelfth grades and asking them who their favorite heroes are, O.J. Simpson came out on top—number one.

The list reflected traditional values, and O.J. Simpson not only won with boys, he was top with girls, too.

The next seven people on the list were, in exact order: Elton John, the rock musician, Neil Armstrong, who had been the first man to land on the moon just seven years before the poll was conducted, John Wayne, the Duke; Robert Redford, the actor; Chris Evert, the tennis star; Mary Tyler Moore; and another tennis star, Billie Jean King.

Politicians ranked low, the tops among kids was Henry Kissinger, who ranked ninth. Then-President Ford ranked a meager thirteenth. Linda Lovelace, the porn star; and Charles Manson, the cult killer; finished fortieth and forty-fourth respectively.

Visibility was the key to O.J.'s success, he parlayed an impressive college football career at the University of Southern California into phenomenal pro football careers with the Buffalo Bills and later the 49ers. After that, each of his goals off the playing field fell like dominoes—the endorsements, the broadcasting contract, the movies, television.

The endorsements came early, back at USC he got a few. By the mid-1970s he was a huckster for RCA, Tree-Sweet Products, Acme Boots, Dingo Boots, Hyde Athletic Industries and Spot-Bilt athletic shoes. He won a lucrative product endorsement contract from General Motors, becoming a spokesman for Chevrolet. At that period he also became the "mouthpiece" for Schick Shavers, Royal Crown Cola (Back on Potrero Hill, Simpson briefly worked as a truck driver for the RC Cola—his estimated $140,000 endorsement deal with them was quite a hefty salary increase from his delivery days.), Wilson Sporting Goods and Foster-Grant Sunglasses.

His winning smile and obvious good-looks was his best selling point—his performance on the football field was the key, his handsome sex appeal opened the door. It was O.J. Simpson behind those Foster-Grants.

His most lucrative, and most durable endorsement contract made Simpson a pop culture icon. The jokes have already begun, jokes about the Juice running through the airport on the night of June 12th, jumping over barriers and charging past other passengers to catch his flight to Chicago. These jokes are as cruel as they are inevitable.

"Hertz, don't it?"

It was a multi-million-dollar, decade long ad campaign for Hertz Rental Cars that imprinted the image of O.J. Simpson running, running, running—even more than on the playing field, O.J.'s runs for Hertz over the years have rewarded the superstar handsomely.

In 1976, at the annual three-day Hertz Corporation convention in Miami, hot and tired executives who had been going at it for nine hours were told that there was yet another speaker to hear from. Five hundred throats issued a collective groan.

The house lights dimmed, and a spotlight beamed from high in the auditorium and O.J. Simpson bounded across the room and up to the podium.

"They went absolutely crazy," Frank A. Olsen, an executive vice-president and general manager of the Hertz Rent a Car division told Rona Cherry of the *New York Times*.

"I've never seen grown people act that way before. It took ten minutes for O.J. to work his way to the stage, and they wouldn't let him go until he had talked for more than forty minutes."

O.J. spoke in a rambling fashion, about his life, his pro football career, but after awhile his tone shifted, and he began to deliver a pep talk on why he liked Hertz, how he was putting his reputation on the line for the company and how everybody in the room should work hard for their company, too. It was a canned speech, but O.J. delivered it with such charming sincerity that this room full of corporate executives—not the most starry-eyed people in the world—were swept away.

He received a standing ovation.

"The enthusiastic reaction to Mr. Simpson helps explain why the officials of Hertz, a subsidiary of the RCA Corporation, are smiling these days," Ms. Cherry wrote.

"Ever since Hertz teamed up with its grid-iron celebrity two years ago in an advertising campaign, both the company and Mr. Simpson have captured public attention with unusually successful results."

The image of O.J. running through an airport, not wearing his familiar number "32" or carrying a football, but dressed to the nines in a three-piece business suit and carrying a briefcase, amounted to what Ms. Cherry called "a different image" being created. It was more than an image, for O.J.

proved to be as adept at business as he was at athletics.

"Once regarded by many people principally as a hard-driving super-athlete, he has been homogenized into a smooth, articulate product promoter," Cherry continued." Now, along with football fans, people who don't know a goalie from a goalpost press him eagerly for his autograph."

The executives at Hertz knew that they had made a wise decision in the two years following the signing of O.J. Simpson as their spokesman.

"He exemplifies the concepts of speed, reliability and efficiency, which happen to be the qualities the company wants to project about itself," Mona Cherry wrote in 1976.

A Hertz spokesman said of O.J., "The perception of O.J. as being with your company makes your message about speed and reliability more believable."

O.J. initially wondered why Hertz approached him.

"They had a slogan—the Superstar in Rent-a-Car—and I was the current reigning superstar as far as the competition was concerned," Simpson told *The New York Times*. Hertz, said O.J., paid him "between $100,000 and $250,000 a year for his Hertz work."

O.J. himself was not surprised by his success as a promoter—and why should he be—it was something that he worked hard for, planned for, and was determined to do the best possible job. Speaking frankly about his appeal as a commercial spokesman, Simpson told a reporter in 1976, "People identify with me and I don't think I'm that offensive to anyone." He also spoke about his race, which he felt neither harmed nor helped him grab product endorsements.

"People have told me I'm colorless," he said. "Everyone likes me. I stay out of politics, I don't try to save people for the Lord and, besides, I don't look that out of character in a suit."

He certainly did not, because he wasn't stepping out of character. The business world suited O.J. to a T.

Hertz was always a company aware, and concerned about, the public's attitude toward it, and a company spokesman told Mona Cherry that they felt that the gridiron superstar's image, which Simpson himself characterized as not "offensive" and "colorless" worked well for them.

"Since Mr. Simpson started the campaign there has been a thirty-six percent increase in the number of people who rate Hertz as 'best' among car-rental companies.''

The Hertz Corporation's share of the marketplace, at the one hundred largest airports in the nation, all posted gains in the two years following the signing of Simpson. According to company officials, "the (Simpson ad campaign) played an important role in attracting customers.''

Even the competition conceded. "The campaign could possibly have hurt us, although I can't be sure,'' said an Avis spokesman.

JUICE, BOOTS AND SPEECHES

In that period of his career, his second most lucrative commercial contract was with Tree-Sweet orange juice company—playing on his nickname—which not only netted Simpson one million dollars for five years, but offered him a percentage of sales in those five years.

Another contract, with Acme Boot Company and their Dingo Boot division, featured magazine and newspaper print ads showing "The Juice" wearing a pair of Dingos with a three-piece suit, or a pair of tight jeans and a nice shirt. The caption read: "He's a Dingo man down to his feet. And when he starts walkin', people start talkin'. Because he walks in the fast lane, and he's all legs. There's a Dingo boot to fit the way *you* dress, the way *you* live.

"So follow O.J.'s lead, and get in step. With Dingo."

Marilyn O'Brien of Sports Headliners, Inc., O.J.'s business manager in the mid-1970s, told Mona Cherry of *The New York Times* that his endorsement contracts were mostly "six-figure involvements," though both O'Brien and Simpson declined to elaborate further. This endorsement money, in addition to his Bills' salary, which at the time was "between one million and substantially less than 2.5 million dollars," made the poor kid from Potrero Hill into a multi-millionaire, a human money machine, before he was thirty years old.

When he became the highest paid athlete in pro football, O.J. was somewhat defensive about his salary from the Bills, but he managed to couch most of his statements in the plural, including *all* pro football players in his defense.

"We deserve good money for playing football," he told a New York reporter in 1977.

"Players have to be realistic about their limited careers. And today we think about that. So we go after a bigger share of the pot now. Why shouldn't we?"

Sports writers can't argue with that. Baseball players average twice the salaries of football players, and their careers can go far beyond that of a gridiron athlete. And football players are much more likely to suffer career-ending, and even permanently debilitating injuries.

There are other, less publicized ways for a sports legend to make money—one way was the banquet speaking circuit. Marilyn O'Brien told Peter Wood for an article in *The New York Times Magazine*, published December 14, 1975, that O.J. "could dine out from now until next Christmas on his backlog of invitations as after-dinner speaker . . . an art form of which, after years of receiving awards and attending banquets, he has become a smooth and confident master" with fees at that time for a single speech reaching $7,500—a fee that would increase to over $10,000 by 1980.

THE MILLIONAIRE

So what was O.J. worth by the end of the 1970s?

You couldn't get an answer from "The Juice". He told the New York *Daily News* in

1977, that, "I never talk money. Bob Hope once told me you can only make enemies by discussing money."

There was much dispute about Simpson's personal worth at his divorce settlement in 1979. Harry Fain, Marguerite's divorce attorney, felt that the settlement should be a hefty one because at that time O.J. was earning $773,000 a year from the 49ers on top of what was fast becoming his primary source of income—movies, commercial endorsements and broadcasting.

O.J.'s commercials for Hertz even came up at his divorce trial, which "The Juice" did not attend.

"I presume Mr. Simpson was held up at the airport jumping over all those signs," the judge said in a sly reference to the Rent-a-Car commercials.

Later on, Marguerite Simpson expressed some bitterness over her final settlement. A year after their divorce was finalized, Marguerite was back in court, asking Los Angeles Superior Court to penalize her ex-husband by setting aside the agreement under which they reportedly split over three million dollars in assets.

Such a move was unprecedented and divorce lawyers contended at the time that it was the first incident in memory that a judge has been asked to set aside a major Hollywood divorce. The motion was launched, not by Harry Fain, Marguerite's first lawyer, but by Marvin G. Cohen, a high powered talent in the litigation field, who assailed the original settlement his client agreed to sign just a year before.

"Extreme pressure was put on her by O.J. and his lawyer, and others to sign the original agreement and get it over with," Marvin Cohen told the *New York Post* on September 3, 1980. He also stressed that in court documents a property agreement may be set aside or modified.

Some of the pressure to end the litigation the year before was no doubt due to the grief that Marguerite Simpson experienced because of the death of her youngest child, who drowned just a few weeks before she agreed to the original terms of the divorce. The phrase "extreme pressure was put on her by O.J." begs the question, did he kept his head while the others around him lost theirs.

THE SPOKESMAN

Of his business style, much has been written, but little revealed. You have to read between the lines to get the real Simpson, the

CEO of Simpson, Inc. His seems to be a "hands-on" managerial style. He told Kay Gardella in July of 1977, that he "likes handling his own business affairs. Even at the time he graduated from college and was approached to do commercials he wisely said he'd become a spokesman for a company but not merely an actor in a commercial."

The difference might seem a subtle one to those unschooled in the way of advertising, but it is a very important difference nonetheless. A commercial actor, if he is a celebrity, can command about $50,000 to $75,000 to do a commercial. Add that to the residuals received when the commercial is aired, and a popular celebrity with a long-running commercial might net between $100,000 and $125,000 on a given commercial.

But if one becomes a celebrity spokesman, then there is an annual salary involved—upwards of $200,000—and you still get paid to make commercials, and the residuals when the commercial is aired. The company has a stake in the celebrity involved, and wants to forge a link in the minds of consumers between their company and the company's spokesman—which means that the commercials filmed will get played more than the average commercial featuring an actor and not a spokesman. Then there are the print ads, the personal appearances for the company, etc., which the celebrity gets reimbursed for as well. Best of all, companies actually pay the celebrity to keep his face in front of the public, so it is much like having your own public relations experts working for you—and the company pays. It's a win-win situation.

And O.J., ever the competitor on and off the athletic field, likes to win.

He continued to be a winner after he left football. While many athletes fade away like old soldiers, O.J. seemed to grow in stature. Near the end of his athletic career, O.J. told Ricki Fulman of the New York *Daily News* that he was pushing so hard to make money because "I plan to retire from football in two years." He was worried that like a lot of athletes, he would fall by the wayside after a few years, forgotten by his once-adoring fans and the huge corporations that previously sought his endorsement. That was one reason he was working on his acting career—the other, of course, was that he really liked acting, and he was serious about it.

As with his junior college days, where he turned down lucrative offers from lesser schools and waited an extra year in limbo

for his break with the University of Southern
California Trojans, O.J. was willing to bide
his time until just the right offer—the right
moment—came along.

Simpson told Fulman, "I had lots of offers
to star in films and play myself early in my
football career.

"But I knew I wasn't ready for that. I
wanted to work with the best actors and learn.
My reviews have all been good, and I have
worked as hard as anybody.

"Football may have opened the doors for
me, but I don't think any actor could have
done any better."

As the "Era of Greed and Excess"—the
1980s—kicked in, O.J. Simpson was still very
much in the public eye. His movie career had
waned somewhat, but he was still going great
guns in other arenas. He managed a portfolio
of investments, and he had a long-term relationship with Hertz that netted him around a
half a million dollars a year in spokesman
salaries and commercial acting. He had
formed Orenthal Productions with NBC, and
kept producing moderately successful made-
for-television and cable television ventures. He
held property in the most exclusive and tony
neighborhoods of Southern California.

Hardly a month went by without O.J. Simpson being mentioned in the newspapers and tabloids. He was producing something, he was starring in something, he was *here*, he was *there*. By now, through his ubiquitous Hertz commercials and a half-dozen other endorsement deals, he was a pop culture icon. Andy Warhol's *Interview* magazine had talked to him in Mexico, he even did talk shows occasionally.

He announced a deal to produce and star in a cable television series with fellow Heisman Trophy winner and USC running back, Marcus Allen. Six episodes were produced. The show was called *Training Camp,* and O.J. played the coach of the team—Allen portrayed a rookie player.

There were lows as well. In 1980, O.J. was scheduled to go to the Moscow Olympics with NBC sports as one of the network anchors. He had already acted as co-anchor for several events during the 1976 Olympics for ABC, but he was not happy with his performance, and felt that he was then still "wet behind the ears." O.J. planned to do a much better job in Moscow. It was something he anticipated eagerly, but it was not to be.

The 1980 invasion of Afghanistan by Soviet forces, and the economic sanctions imposed on the Soviet Union in the aftermath of this rash military action effectively canceled the Olympics, at least as far as the United States was concerned. O.J. had to content himself with several sports specials.

In 1983, after his contract with NBC expired, "The Juice" signed a lucrative contract with ABC, his second with that network. Again he was set to be an anchor on *Monday Night Football*. He replaced Fran Tarkenton, a man that most of the industry insiders thought was just not up to the job. O.J. was set to announce games with Howard Cosell and Frank Gifford.

He actually made his ABC network debut in an August pre-season game, and Tarkenton moved over to the then-popular ABC show, *That's Incredible*. O.J.'s spokesman told the New York *Daily News* that Simpson was "very excited about getting back into football," adding, "he misses it very much." He made his pro-game debut on ABC on September 5th's Dallas-at-Washington game, and a year later he was joined in the broadcast booth by Joe Namath.

But less than three years later, due to sagging ratings and the increasing cost of broadcasting NFL games, ABC had a change of heart. Both Namath and Simpson were removed from the anchor team and Frank Gifford was bumped down to game analyst.

ABC/Capital Cities, in the process of cutting costs, bought out Namath's contract for "less than one million, but more than $800,000," according to an unnamed source within the network structure.

The New York Times for March 25, 1986 reported that Simpson was "offered a position opposite Keith Jackson on the network's coverage of college football."

O.J. was to replace Frank Broyles on college telecasts. Gifford was replaced by Al Michaels. According to ABC, even though *Monday Night Football* had a rise in ratings for the 1985/86 seasons, "the network's total sports operations reportedly lost between $30 million and $50 million a year."

Al Brodsky, an ABC spokesman, told *The Times* that "Professional football is not making money for all three networks.

"We are still interested in it, though the contract has to be equitable from both sides."

Football was to continue a downward trend throughout the 1980's, only the Super Bowl games are guaranteed winners today.

INTO THE HALL OF FAME

In 1985, O.J. was to return to pro football once again, but this time he was not on the playing field, this time he was strutting his stuff as a proud new inductee of the Pro Football Hall of Fame.

On August 3, 1985, O.J. Simpson was inducted into the Hall of Fame in Canton, Ohio. His fellow inductees were Pete Rozelle, Roger Staubach, and his old salary competitor, Joe Namath. Typical of O.J.'s public face, the Hall-of-Fame inductee gave an acceptance speech that was dignified and modest.

"I'm thriller to be included with players like Joe and Roger," he said. In the honors speeches, mention was made of his past career highs—of his 1968 Heisman Trophy win, his spectacular college career for Southern Cal, and his equally spectacular NFL career which spanned eleven seasons and included four rushing titles, five consecutive 1,000 yard seasons and five Pro Bowl selections. There was talk about his eleven-season rushing total of 11,236 yards, and Simpson himself made no mention of the bitterness he once expressed over Walter Payton and Franco Harris beating Brown's rushing record.

Mention was made of the fact that Heisman Trophy winners seldom made it to the Hall of Fame—O.J. and Staubach were the first—and some sports writers have likened the Heisman to the kiss of death.

Much of the focus of Simpson's acceptance speech was his on his mother, Eunice, who attended the ceremony. He spoke about a time when his mother had interrupted her Las Vegas vacation to drive him back to San Francisco for a game.

"She drove me seven hundred miles," he said.

"All the way back to San Francisco in the middle of her vacation so I wouldn't miss my first Little League game."

O.J. spoke about his mother's hard work, and sacrifice, concluding with, "I love you for that . . ." O.J., and half the other people in the room, including his mother, were moved to tears.

But O.J. also addressed the changing nature of football, and the changing reputation of its athletes. Simpson spoke about Joe Namath, who emerged as the symbol of projecting the football player as a "real person."

Simpson called Namath, "a Godsend for all us players" because the Jets' superstar forced people to see the real man under the hero.

"People started to realize that players

didn't always drink milk and eat apple
pie . . .

"I remember reading Joe saying that he
liked his women blond and his Johnny
Walker red. I loved that . . . if we didn't
hurt anyone, we could be ourselves."

As the Hall-of-Fame ceremonies wound
down, and the players and celebrants departed, one sports writer quipped that O.J.
shared another interest with Namath besides
football. It seemed that O.J. Simpson also
liked his women blond.

The journalist was looking across the room
at the very young, very blond, very pregnant
Nicole Brown Simpson.

Ten

Nicole Brown's name first cropped up in connection with O.J. Simpson's almost a year before the gridiron star was divorced from Marguerite. In gossip columns on both coasts, the statuesque blond was variously described as a "beauty queen," a "model," or an "actress." In reality, she was none of these things.

Nicole Brown was an eighteen-year-old high-school senior from Laguna Beach, the Homecoming Queen at the Dana Hills High prom. They met in June, 1977, and by Nicole's own account, they began dating almost immediately. By the time she was nineteen, they were living together. O.J. was thirty.

Before his highly-publicized divorce from his first wife, who gave O.J. three children, Simpson maintained a carefully-controlled public persona—some would say a public mask.

In interview after interview, Simpson would give amazingly consistent statements about his past, his life with Marguerite and his children, and his relationship with teammates and other pro football players. Sometimes he used the same phrases, and the anecdotes sounded almost "canned." Occasionally, there were those incidents when two accounts of his life story would differ, and these incidents could be very revealing.

O.J. certainly gave very conflicting stories about his life as a "street punk" to *Sports Illustrated* and *Playboy.*

In the December, 1976, *Playboy* interview, he gave several accounts of his scrapes with the law during his teenage years that led the reader to believe that he was basically a good kid who went astray occasionally—and that the things he did were more mischievous than malicious.

On the other hand, a *Sports Illustrated* piece for May 11, 1987—an article later condensed for *Reader's Digest*—he told very different stories, tales of underage drinking binges, theft at liquor stores when he was only thirteen or fourteen years old, as well as general shoplifting.

While he did offer a caveat of sorts to *Playboy,* stating, he "didn't want to make himself look too good," he nevertheless glossed over or misstated facts to soften his tale of arrest for a liquor store shoplifting spree. In the

Playboy story, he begged his friends not to steal the liquor. In the *Sports Illustrated* story he portrayed himself as an active participant in the crime.

The discrepancies were mild, but they were there. O.J. probably wasn't intentionally lying, he was merely guarding his public persona—his squeaky clean image was, after all, his livelihood. If pro football didn't much care if the players' womanized, or drank to excess after the games—companies who paid plenty of money to buy an athletes reputation *did* care, and cared very much.

Hertz, by their own admission, bought O.J.'s "reliability," "efficiency," not to mention his good-looks and pleasant disposition. O.J.'s reputation was his stock and trade.

O.J. had another quality that endeared him to his many acquaintances, and the people he came in contact with in his day-to-day working life. He was sometimes self-deprecating in that he always made others feel like they were something special. O.J. might have been the gridiron legend, the movie star, the millionaire, but he never put on airs in public. This humility, sincere or otherwise, infuriated at least one of O.J.'s closest friends—football legend Jim Brown.

In Jim Brown's autobiography, *Out of*

Bounds, the former Cleveland Browns running back and the man who held onto the lifetime running record "The Juice" could never—or was never given a chance—to break. Brown was very candid about what it takes to be a running back.

"Because they are judged by a higher standard, great runners must think, 'I Am Superior' . . . all the top runners have felt the same way.

"That included O.J. Simpson. 'The Juice' likes to pretend he's modest, but that's just 'The Juice', *being* 'The Juice'. O.J. is extremely smart, the man knows how to make a buck, and his 'aw shucks' image is his meal ticket. He's not about to jeopardize it by being honest."

Brown offers an example of what he's talking about.

"I was watching 'The Juice' announce a game once, he said the guy down on the field was probably a finer runner than he'd been.

"What a bunch of bullshit! I know O.J. Simpson. He doesn't think there's a runner, dead or alive, who was a better back than he was."

The former Cleveland Browns Hall-of-Famer was quick to stress that "I basically like 'The Juice'," then went on to add:

"I never look at him the way I do a Bill

Russell, or a Walter Payton. I talk to those guys, see them speak, I know what I'm hearing is the real man. Too often, I can't say the same about O.J."

Was O.J. *"being* 'The Juice' " when he talked about his domestic life with Marguerite?

In his *Playboy* interview, he spoke disparagingly about rumors of womanizing. He claimed he never had a "plethora of groupies." Yet after his marriage, in a March, 1979, *Cosmopolitan* feature article written by John Eskow, he hinted at a very different truth—although he couched his statements in *very* general terms.

"Some people get nearsighted about sex—you see it in athletics. As a man, you grow up, the ultimate thing is to get laid.

"Now you've made it in athletics, you're layin' everybody—so what else is there? Hopefully, it's just a phase. It *is* bred into the minds of men to get a lot of women, and every man capable of it has to go through that phase."

Only at the end of this section of the interview does he slip back into his persona as "The Juice".

"Throughout my youth, despite the fact that I was thought to be a playboy, I really wasn't. But I like the image. Even so, being in sports, I had to focus on that."

In that same interview, O.J. spoke of his recent television movie, "The Killing Affair," with some enthusiasm.

"I've only had one real *part*—in the CBS movie "A Killing Affair," with Elizabeth Montgomery. That was the first time I played a real guy, and I had to make him a good guy. After all, this was a black guy screwing around on his wife with a white lady—on television! I enjoyed that challenge."

This made-for-television film was made only a year or so before O.J. separation from his first wife, and the beginning of his relationship with Nicole Brown.

Was it a case of method acting?

Though no "other woman" was named in the Marguerite Simpson/Orenthal James Simpson divorce—the reason for the split was cited as "irreconcilable differences"—Marguerite was somewhat candid in an interview she gave for a book called *Superwives*.

In this 1976 book, Marguerite complained bitterly at about how both football and her husband's other commitments took him away from hearth and home for too many months out of the year. She also told the author that "I have been shoved out of the way, pushed and stepped on by more than one beautiful woman."

She was also honest enough to admit that she felt threatened by the attention women were showering her husband with, and was "jealous." But was she speaking about the groupies, the hangers-on, the kind of women who threw themselves at celebrities—the kind of woman O.J. belittled, stating that he was unimpressed with groupies, and just "didn't see them" in the *Cosmopolitan* article—or was she hinting at more than that?

The interview for *Superwives* was conducted at a time when their separation—he was playing in Buffalo, she was living in Bel Air—was taking its toll on their marriage. It was also during this period that an unidentified friend—probably Al Cowlings—told *Sports Illustrated* that "If O.J. does not make a concentrated effort right now, the marriage will end."

Certainly O.J. *did* make that "concentrated effort" but it simply wasn't enough. He was given an impossible choice, forced to decide between his family and his career—a decision no one should have to make, yet most of us make every single day. O.J. chose football, and lost his marriage.

Did the tabloid rumors about O.J. and a

tall, sexy blond push Marguerite over the edge and drive her to divorce court?

There is a story published in the October 29, 1973, issue of *Sports Illustrated*, that is either ironic, prophetic, or revealing, depending on one's take on it.

The story, aptly titled "Now You See Him, Now You Don't" concerns O.J.'s Buffalo days, and was written by Joe Marshall:

"Not long ago Simpson was cooling his heels in Mulligan's Museum of Fine Arts and Cafe, a Buffalo discotheque.

"He lit a cigarette, not because he smokes—he doesn't—but because it was a John Player Special, which he had never seen before and because the cigarettes came in a snappy box. O.J. likes snappy things . . .

"Simpson took a puff of the John Player Special, holding it delicately between the ends of his thumb and forefinger, tilting his head back like a connoisseur. 'Yes,'" he said, 'that's pretty good.'

" 'You're going to get sick," said Marguerite.

"Attention focused elsewhere, but O.J. faces a crisis. A long ash had formed on his cigarette, and not being a smoker he was unsure

how best to dispose of it. Carefully he poised
the cigarette over an ashtray, then flicked at
the center of it with his middle finger. The
cigarette shot out of his hand, somersaulted
in the air and landed beside the ashtray. He
looked quickly around the table to see if anybody had noticed. He thought he was safe until he confronted the last possible witness, who
met his stare with a big smile. O.J. burst out
laughing. He laughed even harder at himself
while the others listened to the witness' description of his gaucherie."

We can see how image conscious O.J. was
even at this early stage of his football career.
He didn't want to look like a fool. And the
phrase, "O.J. likes flashy things," particularly, sticks in one's mind with regard to Nicole Brown.

Despite their loving and passionate relationship, O.J. and Nicole postponed marriage for a long time. They were married in
all but the legal sense by the time she was
nineteen. In reality, Nicole Brown was practically living with him. At that very same
time, O.J. was still married to his first wife,
Marguerite, who had given birth to Aaren
Simpson, the daughter who drowned a few

days before her second birthday, less than three months *after* Simpson and Nicole met.

The timing here raises a number of questions—for one thing, was O.J. sleeping with Nicole while he was still legally married? Was he carrying on an affair with Nicole, even while his wife was pregnant and waiting to give birth to their third child?

After the divorce, O.J. and Nicole lived life in the fast lane. Though "The Juice" had to part with at least one and a half and possibly two million dollars in the divorce settlement, he was still phenomenally wealthy, and he and Nicole live in extraordinary luxury.

Nicole dropped out of junior college to, she maintained, be with O.J. when he traveled. Nicole was very different from his first wife, who spoke of O.J.'s love of domestication, and who would rather stay home and raise their two children than go on the road with O.J. and the Bills. Nicole liked travel, she liked excitement, and she liked being on the arm of this stunningly handsome and fantastically wealthy celebrity who was beloved and idolized by millions.

Those who knew Nicole spoke of her vivacious personality, her sunny disposition, her undeniable attractiveness. Nobody spoke of her drive, her ambition, her ultimate goal or goals in life. If she had a career path in mind, she never pursued it. In the divorce motion Nicole filed against O.J. in 1992, she demanded a huge property and alimony settlement.

Her lawyer told the judge that his client had almost no work history and no skills. Except for brief stints as a waitress in a tony restaurant, and a sales clerk in an upscale boutique, she never worked, "except perhaps as an interior decorator for Simpson and his wealthy friends," as one unnamed acquaintance put it.

It seems that even before their marriage, Nicole Brown was perfectly content to live on the incredible wealth that O.J.'s hard work provided.

That wealth encompassed the Brentwood mansion which was worth an estimated five to seven million dollars and included a full staff of servants; and an oceanfront house in Laguna Beach, Nicole's home town, worth an estimated two million dollars. According to newspaper reports, the Laguna Beach property was only used in the summer and never rented out to others—though O.J. or Nicole did occasionally make the residence available to friends and family. There were trips on private jets, shopping trips mostly, not to mention monthly "pocket money" to the

tune of $5,000 or $6,000 a month, which
O.J. freely gave to Nicole.

The Simpsons also vacationed in Hawaii,
every single year. The trip was usually an all-
expenses paid affair given to the Simpson family as a perk from Hertz—so O.J. could
promote the company and attend their executive meetings and other corporate functions.

O.J. and Nicole also enjoyed a bicoastal lifestyle—so, to facilitate that, in 1990, the Simpsons purchased a five-room condo in the
Bristol Plaza on East 65th Street, on Manhat-
tan's posh Upper East Side. This love nest
cost them over a million dollars. There were
his and her Ferraris, more modest vehicles on
both coasts, annual skiing trips to Aspen, and
Vail. They liked to frequent trendy nightspots
and the best restaurants on both coasts. In
New York, O.J. stopped at the Harley Davidson Cafe, or the Dakota Bar & Grill.

Nicole, it was said, liked to cook and en-
tertain, and she provided the cuisine for
every one who attended their huge, celebrity-
packed parties.

O.J. admitted that he, like other athletes,
drank and even smoked occasionally—but, as
with the tales of womanizing he related to
Cosmopolitan, he couched these admissions in
very general, even impersonal, terms.

In a talk he had with a reporter from Andy Warhol's trendy magazine, *Interview*, O.J. said:

"Athletes drink and smoke more than anybody, as much as rock singers or anybody. So don't let anyone tell you they don't.

"Why? Because my game is based totally on competition, so let's face it, the harder you work under a pressure situation, the harder you're gonna play when you're not under pressure.

"You gotta let it all out in order to live . . .

"Christ, when the game's over and you see the cats, they go out and put away Scotches and beer and, hey, you gotta have sex, too . . .

"And the better shape you're in, the more you crave it."

Later, as certain facts emerged concerning his domestic situation with Nicole, people would begin to question his image—but that was still a few years away.

O.J. got his first taste of "reverse racism" when, according to a report published in *Ebony* magazine, African-American women became angry over his portrayal of a adulterous black man, cheating on his black wife, with a white woman in "The Killing Affair." He got a second taste of it when, several years later, Nicole Brown became Nicole Brown Simpson on February 2, 1985.

If there was racism involved, according to Jim Brown, it was probably coming from both sides. In his 1989 book, *Out of Bounds*, Brown discussed O.J., his two marriages, and the pitfalls of interracial marriage.

"A black man who messes with white women, especially if that black man has no economic power, still takes a gamble in this country.

"O.J. Simpson did it. he left his first wife, Marguerite, who is black, later married the lady he's with now, who is white. As image-oriented as "The Juice" is, that surprised me. Now in those corporate boardrooms, "The Juice" isn't quite so All-American. They didn't blackball him, didn't take away his commercials, but you can bet he heard about it, or felt it, on some scale, in one guise or another."

If there was any fallout from O.J.'s interracial romance, it didn't seem to bother him. In fact, he stated more than once that he liked to break racial barriers, and was proud of his role in "The Killing Affair." He told *Interview* magazine that the role in this drama was "the type of stuff I'm looking for. It's challenging."

O.J. had proposed to Nicole, and gave her an engagement ring in 1982, but they were having too much fun to rush to the altar. The couple lived together for almost seven years before they finally tied the knot. They married in O.J.'s Brentwood mansion, and celebrated with another celebrity-filled bash attended by almost four hundred of their closest friends and family members, including O.J.'s daughter Arnelle Simpson, fifteen, and son Jason, thirteen, from his first marriage.

Ten months after the wedding, Nicole gave birth to the first of the couple's two children. Sydney, a daughter, was born on October 17. Two years later Nicole was pregnant again, and their son Justin was born August 6, 1988.

It wasn't long before O.J. was back to his old ways—or repeating family history, as modern twelve-step therapists would term it—he was soon working and traveling more than he was home. Nicole, stuck with the almost exclusive care of the two children, could not join him as much as she used to, and tension began to creep into their marriage. Like his father, O.J. became, in both his first marriage and his second, very much of an absentee parent. Even when he was home, Nicole complained to family and friends that he spent only a few hours each day with his two children.

Like O.J.'s mother Eunice, and like his
first wife Marguerite, Nicole was left holding
the bag—and raising the children.

The public facade remained the same.
They attended parties together, traveled
when Nicole could manage it, and were seen
in each others' company often. The bicoastal
lifestyle continued as well, though as Sydney
began school it became harder to disrupt her
education for jaunts to New York.

The couple and their children still managed to make their Hawaii trip yearly, and
the still entertained with lavish parties—
though friends report that they threw bashes
less frequently.

Nicole belonged to an upscale health club
called The Gym, and frequented many restaurants in the Brentwood and Santa Monica
area. The willowy blond was a familiar sight
in Brentwood, tooling around in her white
Ferrari convertible, sometimes with the children in tow, sometimes on her own.

She still liked to shop, and she was a flashy,
yet tasteful dresser. Her two sisters were frequent visitors to the Brentwood mansion, and
often kept Nicole company when O.J. was out
of town. She often spent time with her family
when she visited the oceanfront home in
Laguna Beach during the summer months.

They were a typical, albeit fabulously wealthy, married couple with the stereotypical two children. No one who saw them together could have imagined that there was a dark secret hidden from the public eye, a secret that ~uld—if the Los Angeles authorities are cor- in their charges against the former super- eventually reach out and destroy them

The first sign of trouble in the Simpson's paradise in Brentwood arrived in 1989, with the new year. It was the first news of domestic discord between Nicole and O.J. to reach the public. The events in question occurred after a New Year's Eve party that O.J. and Nicole attended the night of December 31, 1988, less than four months after the birth of their second child.

At about 2:45 A.M., according to various published reports, the police were summoned to the couple posh Brentwood estate by a frantic 911 call. When a black-and-white patrol car arrived, the police found the gate locked. They rang a security button at the locked gate several times before an unnamed housekeeper arrived.

The police were told to go away by the

housekeeper, but they insisted on entering the compound. Then, emerging from some bushes, shaking with fear and wearing only a bra and sweatpants, Nicole ran up to the police and opened the gate. Police reports say that the cops found her with her face bruised, scratches on and handprints on her neck and her lips was swollen. She ran up to one of the officers, called Edwards in the published reports, yelling "He's going to kill me, he's going to kill me!"

"Who's going to kill you?" asked the uniformed officer.

"O.J.'s going to kill me, he beat me up."

"O.J.? Do you mean O.J. Simpson the football player?"

"Yes." Nicole shouted, still shaking.

"Okay," the officer soothed, "you're all right now."

The Nicole began shouting again.

"You never do anything about him. You talk to him and they you leave. I want him arrested. I want him out so I can get my kids."

Then O.J. appeared and began arguing with the cops and yelling at Nicole, who was sitting in the patrol car. When one officer told O.J. that he was about to be arrested, he got angrier.

"The police have been here eight times before and now you're gonna arrest me for this?" the gridiron legend screamed.

"This is a family matter," he shouted, why do you want to make a big deal out of it?"

Then Simpson walked—or ran—to his 1981, blue Rolls Royce Bentley and drove away. The police report states that the officers gave chase but were unsuccessful at capturing him—it wouldn't be the first time.

Nor was it the first time that the police were called, as it was later reported after the events of June, 1994. Simpson was arrested later that day, and was charged with assault.

In the subsequent days after the murder of Nicole Simpson, the press was rife with stories that O.J. had indeed beaten his wife in several incidents, and threatened her in others. There was at least one documented incident in which Nicole made a tearful call to 911. On the tape, made October 25, 1993, the voice of the Hall of Fame running back can be heard shouting obscenities because he had seen photos of an ex-boyfriend in her photo album.

As a result of this incident, Nicole required treatment at a local hospital. Four months after the incident, Mr. Simpson pleaded no contest to a charge of spousal abuse, and was sentenced by the judge, Ronald Schoenberg, to 120 hours of community service and two years probation. After the sentencing the couple issued a joint statement that read in part:

"Our marriage is as strong as the day we were married, if not stronger."

In the letter O.J. gave to the press when he was a fugitive from double-murder charges, he stated that he "took the heat New Years 1989, because that's what I was supposed to do.

"I did not plead no contest for any other reason but to protect our privacy, and was advised it would end the press hype." Simpson added that, "At times I have felt like a battered husband or boyfriend, but I loved her."

"The Juice" was sentenced to pay a paltry fine of $200, and was ordered to pay a battered woman's shelter $500. He was also ordered to perform 120 hours of community service, which he did not finish in California, but was permitted by the courts to complete in New York, where he was working to fulfill several broadcast contracts.

Special treatment? Experts said no. While the fines were exceedingly low, few wife beaters serve time in jail, and most are released both before and after sentencing.

Dr. Susan Forward, therapist and author of the book *Men Who Hate Women & The Women Who Love Them*, counseled Nicole Brown

Simpson briefly in 1992. In her opinion, O.J. was a classic violent spouse, who fit the basic descriptions of the case studies in her book.

"He would say to her things like, 'If I can't have you, nobody can, ' " said Dr. Forward on *Hard Copy*.

"To the best of my recollection, she told me of several incidents where he said, 'I'm going to kill you. If I can't have you, I'm going to kill you.' "

"He just wasn't willing to let go. He wanted that woman, and he wanted her back. She'd see him loitering outside the house, looking in the window. He would show up at restaurants or bars where she would be . . . she had no idea how she knew he was going to be there."

On that same broadcast of *Hard Copy*, an anonymous male friend of Nicole's came forward to comment:

"I overheard a conversation with her and her psychiatrist one day, and she was talking about some guy she met and she went out with him and O.J. saw him and he got jealous. And she was telling her psychiatrist, 'Yeah, you know, I like him when he gets that way . . . ' "

In March of 1992, Nicole Brown Simpson filed for a divorce. The papers cited irreconcilable differences, and no mention of do-

mestic violence was mentioned. They had
been together for over fifteen years.

This time, the split was not so amicable. O.J.
provided for Nicole very well financially, and
the settlement netted her a lucrative chunk of
the superstar's assets, but friends report that
O.J. was not happy about losing Nicole.

He launched a determined effort to get
her back. When the Laguna Beach mansion
burned in the 1992 fires in Southern California, O.J. was said to pay for Nicole's re-
location to her Brentwood town house, the
place where she was murdered.

According to news stories published in the
days after Nicole's murder, O. J. was despondent after the divorce. He was frequently seen
with a model named Paula Barbieri, who appeared in the *Victoria's Secret* catalogue and in
Vogue. Paula, through a close friend, issued a
statement that she was not romantically involved with Simpson, but that they were just
"friends."

Sometime in early April, 1994, Simpson asked
Nicole to accompany him to Mexico. She refused. Simpson made the trip alone, and people
who saw him at the hotel in Baja felt he looked

despondent and depressed. The clerk at the hotel said simply that "he was alone."

When he returned to Los Angeles, he took to appearing at the Brentwood town house of his ex-wife and their children unannounced, and at odd hours. He was not always welcome.

On June 12, O.J. attended a dance recital for his daughter, Sydney, where she danced to the tune of *Footloose*. Witnesses said that he asked Nicole if he could sit with her, but his ex-wife refused his request, and he sat a few rows away. After the recital, O.J. joined his family and learned of the dinner party planned at Mezzaluna. He asked to attend, but Nicole again refused. She departed with her children, her two sisters, and five other friends.

O.J. left to prepare for his flight to Chicago on a promotional tour.

The police believe that at that point O.J. had reached the state where anything possible, the police believe that he waited outside of his ex-wife's town house, and when she appeared at the door to get the glasses she'd forgotten at the restaurant—the glasses that the waiter, Ronald Lyle Goodman agreed to stop by and return to her—O.J. struck.

Many of his fans and admirers believe otherwise.

Now O.J. waits for a judge and jury to decide his fate.

Eleven

The Aftermath

A DAY-BY-DAY ACCOUNT OF
THE AFTERMATH OF THE NICOLE
BROWN SIMPSON/RONALD LYLE GOLD-
MAN MURDERS

A chronology of the events as they unfolded in the media after the murder of Nicole Brown Simpson and Ronald Lyle Goodman is as follows:

MONDAY, JUNE 13

The first reports of the murder reached the television news.

The police begin an immediate investigation. O.J. was picked up at his home after he returned from his scheduled trip to Chicago. The sports legend was then handcuffed briefly and grilled by police. The handcuffs were the first signal to the press and public that Simpson might indeed be a suspect.

Throughout the interrogation, Simpson maintains his innocence and ignorance of the events surrounding the terrible crime.

After four hours of questioning, he still denies any knowledge of his wife's murder and is finally released from police custody—

he is not charged. The questioning, said to be "extensive" did not crack O.J. or change his alibi—he was, he maintains, on his way to Chicago and had nothing whatsoever to do with his wife's and Ronald Goldman's murder.

One telling fact later emerged. Police, while examining O.J. during interrogation, found a deep cut on his hand. Later, unconfirmed sources report that this wound could have been inflicted in a struggle.

If O.J. was the killer, could this have occurred when O.J. fought with Goldman? Or even in a struggle with his ex-wife?

Simpson claimed that he hurt his hand when he broke a glass in his Chicago hotel room, after being notified that his wife was dead.

The police said they expected an "early resolution to this case . . . the department was pleased with the cooperation it has received," from Simpson.

Simpson declined to answer questions from the press, stating only that he knew "nothing." Simpson's lawyer, Howard Weitzman, who represented Michael Jackson in his much-publicized child molestation civil suit, told reporters that his client was innocent, that O.J.

first heard of the murders in Chicago, and that he rushed home immediately after that.

Mr. Weitzman said that the estimated time of the killings was eleven p.m. and that Mr. Simpson was probably on his way to the airport at that time, or was already there. At that point in the investigation, Weitzman told the press that his client was not a suspect—which was what the police told the press a few hours before.

Later the authorities changed their story, they then issued a statement indicating that they had "not ruled out anyone."

At a news conference, L.A. Police Commander David Gascon said that Simpson had cooperated with investigators and was being treated as a witness, not a suspect. He stated that police had no information about the state of the couple's relationship prior to the murders—which was patently untrue, for they had only to consult their records for the history of his 1989 arrest and plea of "no contest," and a more recent, tearful call from Nicole to 911 on October 25, 1993.

The Los Angeles Medical Examiner's Office begins an autopsy. Blood and flesh samples acquired at the crime scene are tested, though the results are at first incomplete. DNA testing is time consuming and will take more time to complete.

Scenes of O.J. in handcuffs are broadcast nationwide. The nation is shocked to see the star running back—the Hertz spokesman, the man who sold them orange juice, boots and Foster-Grant sunglasses, who made them laugh on *Saturday Night Live* and in the *Naked Gun* movies—handcuffed and surrounded by ranks of police.

The shocks would continue.

Warrants to search O.J. Simpson's house, the grounds around the mansion, the guest houses and the vehicles owned by the celebrity are obtained. The search warrants yield more evidence, seemingly damning evidence of Simpson's guilt in the murders.

TUESDAY, JUNE 14

Stunning new details of the murders are revealed, mostly through leaks to the press and often through unsubstantiated and even untrue suppositions and rumors.

* * *

Los Angeles police await the results of the forensic tests. News leaks that O.J. Simpson's arrest was "imminent."

The first reports of physical evidence reach the press. The reports which surface indicate that a bloodied glove is found at the murder scene, and another, which matched it, was found on O.J. Simpson's multi-million dollar estate.

There is news of bloodstains found inside of one of O.J.'s many cars—a white Ford Bronco that matched the vehicle that a jogger would later claim to see parked in front of Nicole Simpson's townhouse on the night of the murders.

A ski mask is found, and is said to be "bloody." Is the blood fresh? Police and authorities still have not commented about either the glove or the ski mask.

Howard Weitzman denies that authorities found any "bloodied glove." Weitzman continued to maintain that his client was innocent, and also denied leaks to the press which suggest that there were bloodstains found in Simpson's car and on his driveway, even though televised reports show the police examining the driveway, and several mysterious brownish-red stains are clearly visible to the cameras. A pair of the ex-football star's white Reeboks, confiscated by the police on Monday are examined and compared with footprints found at the murder scene.

The white Ford Bronco, which was impounded on Monday, is given a thorough examination at a police garage.

Friends and relatives of O.J. Simpson visit him at his home. Buffalo Bills teammate Bob Chandler and singer Jermaine Jackson filed in and out of the superstars home that day, wishing him well and expressing their sorrow for his loss and their belief that he is innocent and will be cleared of all innuendoes of guilt, which fill the newspapers and television shows. Television vans surround O.J.'s Brentwood estate. Visitors to the distraught Simpson home must dodge cameras and pushing journalists demanding a statement. Few offer anything to the press, though one person, an unidentified friend of the superstar, did tell the reporters that O.J. was "very upset and tired."

Dr. Susan Forward, who offered psychological counseling to Nicole Brown Simpson for a very brief period in 1992—two hour-long visits, to be exact—goes public on a Los Angeles television interview.

Dr. Forward called Nicole Simpson "a classic battered wife who was both stalked and threatened by her ex-husband," on this now controversial KCBS interview.

Reports surface that Chicago police searched the room that O.J. briefly stayed in at the O'Hare Plaza-Hotel on Monday and they discovered broken glass and a bloody towel.

It was also learned that Simpson made over a dozen calls from the hotel room in his one hour and fifteen minute stay after he was notified of his wife's murder. The records of those calls were confiscated by the Chicago police at the request of Los Angeles officials.

The Los Angeles Medical Examiner's office issues a report stating that Nicole Simpson and Ronald Goldman died of "multiple sharp-forced injuries and stab wounds."

An official spokesman would not comment on the type of murder weapon used, nor on reports that the victims' throats were slashed, and said that the LAPD requested that no more information be released until an arrest is made. This request is ignored by someone in the LAPD, for the "leaks" continue.

A journalist from the *Los Angeles Times*, speaking on CNN's *Breaking News* program on the Monday of O.J. Simpson's arraignment, defends the California press from charges of leaking information.

"There are no 'leaks'," the journalist maintains, "only legitimate information obtained from sources that have a long-standing working relationship with the Los Angeles police."

Howard Weitzman also denies that O.J. knew the male victim, Ronald Goldman, who was then reported to have modeled for Giorgio Armani and had "a reputation as a Lothario among the beautiful people in posh Brentwood." Another friend of the Simpsons stated that O.J. was introduced to Goldman before the 1992 divorce and that the waiter/model had actually stayed in guest houses on the couple's property.

Neighbors and acquaintances make statements to the press to the effect that they often saw Nicole in Goldman's company.

A report in the *Los Angeles Times* told of a neighbor who saw the bodies when the police removed the sheets covering them. Nicole was said to be lying on her side and "that there were some abrasions on the side of her face" and that "there was a lot of blood on both bodies."

Outside the townhouse where the murders took place, bouquets of flowers purchased at local florist shops, as well as bunches of wild-flowers gathered from the surrounding area, were beginning to appear, left by grieving neighbors and admirers of the Simpson family.

A still uncleaned pool of blood was visible on the sidewalk. Also outside the townhouse, someone left a letter addressed to the Simpson's two children. It read in part:

"Mothers hold their children's hands for a short while, their hearts forever. God bless you both and may your mother's spirit reside in your hearts forever."

It was signed Adam and Ali and their mom.

People who knew Simpson and his wife Nicole spoke about a thread of violence that seemed to belie Simpson's squeaky-clean, All-American reputation as a gentleman and a superstar.

Vic Caruccci, a Buffalo sportswriter, told

the *New York Daily News* that he "knew there
were tough times.

"Even before the beating story there were
a lot of suppositions and assumptions by
those who knew them that he was doing
nasty things to her."

Reports also surfaced about O.J.'s strange behavior at a party held the day before the murder. Simpson was seen bragging about all the
women he was dating, and sleeping with. It
seemed out of character to several of his
friends, and even shock jock Howard Stern
made mention on his popular radio broadcast
about O.J.'s weird behavior that night.

The "Cindy Adams" column commented on
his behavior at that same party for Jihan
Sadat, the widow of the murdered President
of Egypt, Anwar Sadat. She said he was
"laughing, joking" and one guest was quoted
as saying, "He had a smile from ear-to-ear."
Nikki Haskell of Star Caps Diet Pill fame
said that O.J. looked "very happy to me.

"He sure didn't look like anybody who was
planning to kill his wife."

The LAPD announced that DNA testing
would begin on the bloodstains found at the

scene. Reports were leaked that O.J. was covered with scratches when he was picked up by police for questioning.

News reports first indicated that Simpson also had a cut on his hand, the result, he told police, of shattering a glass when he received the shocking news of his wife's murder in his Chicago hotel room. The Chicago police later confirmed that a broken glass was found in the O'Hare Plaza-Hotel room. This was known by the LAPD on Monday, but the news was not confirmed until Tuesday.

Hertz, which used O.J. Simpson as its spokesperson for over seventeen years, dropped his television ads.

"There's not a company in this country that would touch him," said Marty Blackman of Blackman and Raybar, advertising consultants.

Meanwhile, as a tide of speculation surrounded the superstar running back and commercial pitchman, O.J. Simpson himself remained in seculsion at his home as dozens of friends and supporters continued to visit him and a tide of fans and admirers began to set up a round-the-clock watch, a vigil of sorts, in front of his house.

Dionne Warwick visited, and was said by other friends of O.J.'s to be very supportive.

At this point, to reassure the worried residents of Brentwood, it was quietly "leaked" by police sources that Simpson was the *sole* suspect, that there was no deranged serial killer, no maniac stalking the post suburbs of Los Angeles.

At that point, the circumstantial evidence police had found at Simpson's home and at the scene could have been enough to arrest him then and there. But, for some inexplicable reason the authorities decided to wait.

Were they afraid of another Rodney King situation—were they afraid of the appearance of racism in the case? The riots following the acquittal of the police who beat Rodney King had uncovered a raw and ugly nerve in Los Angeles. Would the Simpson case agitate that wound futher? Could California, could *America*, afford another race riot in Los Angeles?

Detectives decided that only after the blood tests were completed would they make their move. These tests, which would no doubt give them a better idea of whether samples of blood matching O.J.'s blood type were left at the scene, would still not be conclusive.

As for the DNA tests, which had begun

and which would take much longer, only time would tell.

WEDNESDAY, JUNE 15

A new bombshell drops and things get much stranger. Simpson's lawyer, the high-powered attorney Howard Weitzman, quits abruptly, citing he was just "too busy" to defend his client against murder charges.

"I'm much too busy," he says. He also stated he was too close to Simpson to handle the case. Weitzman, who defended Michael Jackson in his civil suit against the child molestation accusations, was considered O.J.'s best defense against any charges of murder which may be filed. Weitzman was widely considered to be one of the best trial lawyers in the country because he was always a "fighter" who worked his magic in the courtroom in front of a jury.

There were others who speculated that Weitzman left the case because he believed Simpson *was* guilty and he didn't want to defend a guilty client and risk defeat.

Backing that particular theory was the emergence of Robert Shapiro to take his place.

***

New lawyer Robert Shapiro quickly changes O.J.'s alibi. Now O.J. was said to be waiting at his Brentwood estate for the limo to arrive and take him to the airport. Shapiro vows to hire the best defense team, including technical experts, to clear his client of wrongdoing.

Unlike Weitzman, the "fighter," Shapiro is considered a "dealmaker," not a trial lawyer. Shapiro is known as a bargaining expert and prefers plea bargaining to fighting it out in court.

Shapiro had previously represented Christian Brando in his murder trial, when the son of the Academy Award-winning star of *The Godfather* was accused of killing his half-sister's lover. The Brando case—which was plea-bargained down to a lesser charge—as well as other high-profile athletes like former Met's baseball player Vince Coleman, and Darryl Strawberry, never went to trial. In Christian Brando's case, Shapiro was so successful that he got the murder charges first reduced to manslaughter, and then got Brando out of jail six years earlier than the judge's original sentence.

F. Lee Bailey, a noted trial lawyer himself,

once hired Shapiro to defend him against drunk driving charges, which were plea-bargained to a lesser charge.

"You hire him when the jig is up and you want to get the lowest possible sentence," stated the *New York Post*.

Meanwhile the police reveal that they have more physical evidence, including "fingerprint, hair fibre and blood samples to be analyzed," Lt. John Dunkin told the press, and Los Angeles television station KNBC. He stated that police had "definitive" physical proof linking Simpson to the crime scene.

The grief-stricken parents and siblings of Ronald Goldman hold a press conference in which they talk about their murdered son.

"He cared about everyone he came in touch with," a sobbing Fred Goldman told the press. "He was a caring friend to all."

"He was open about the gals he dated," the distraught father told the press conference, "If she (Nicole) had been anything more than a friend, we would have known (about it)."

Goldman, who was raised in Chicago by his father after his parents' divorce, was called "a special human being who didn't deserve what happened to him.

"It doesn't surprise me that he would be the person who offered to return Nicole's glasses. She and he were friends."

Dr. Susan Forward, who gave statements about her therapy sessions with Nicole Brown found herself in hot water. The California State Board of Behavioral Science Examiners said yesterday that it may investigate whether Forward violated confidentiality laws.

The tabloid show *Hard Copy* reported that the police asked O.J. Simpson to submit to a lie detector test, but he refused.

The gridiron star remained in seclusion from the press, awaiting the funeral of his murdered wife. He did appear briefly in public on Wednesday, to attend a private ceremony for Nicole Brown Simpson at an Orange County funeral home in Laguna Hills.

At the funeral home, O.J. looked stricken with grief as he knelt at his dead ex-wife's open coffin and mouthed a silent prayer. He leaned close to Nicole's face and wept.

Nicole Brown Simpson lay in state in a dress with a high collar—to cover the wounds on her neck, one report stated. The funeral director would offer no comment on the reconstruction work he was forced to perform to make the late-Mrs. Simpson presentable to the mourners.

THURSDAY, JUNE 16

Two television interviews with the limo driver sent to pick up Simpson contradict the superstar's alibi.

The driver revealed that Simpson may not have been at his home at 10:45 p.m. on the night of the murder. The unidentified driver stated that he picked up a "sweaty and agitated" Simpson at about 11:15 p.m. and drove him to the airport.

This material witness, who had already been interviewed by the police, said that he arrived on time for the pick up, rang the gate and no one appeared after fifteen minutes. He called his dispatcher, who told him to try again, and when he did, a "blond man" opened the gate and let him in. He waited for several minutes and then a "nervous" Simpson arrived.

He stated—in two separate interviews on two tabloid journalism television shows—that

O.J.'s skin appeared damp and he was either "sweating" or had "just taken a shower."

KCAL television in L.A. said that the driver and his supervisor will be key prosecution witnesses.

A woman who stated she was jogging past Nicole Simpson's home in Brentwood on Sunday night came forward and told police detectives that she saw O.J.'s Ford Bronco in the driveway. Police now believe that the victims were slashed and stabbed with a "military-style bayonet," KCOP-TV reported. The search for the murder weapon was continuing.

It is a day for funerals—and the sadness of the affairs is belied by the beautiful Southern California skies that look down on the mourners.

The funeral for Nicole Brown Simpson is held at St. Martin of Tours Catholic Church in Brentwood. Like his first wife Marguerite, Nicole Brown Simpson was raised a Catholic. Scores of mourners file into the church.

Al Cowlings, O.J.'s childhood friend, who followed him on the football field at junior college, at the University of Southern California, and into the pros with the Buffalo

Bills, acted as gatekeeper at the funeral. Cowlings job was keeping out curiosity seekers and allowing those familiar with the Simpsons to pass.

O.J., accompanied by his two children by his marriage to Nicole, had to be supported by friends, his grief was so overwhelming. Wearing a black suit and sunglasses, with tears of grief running down his face and dripping onto his white shirt, he stood at the front row with his two children in hand.

"If he was feeling any guilt, he certainly didn't show it," quipped a reporter for the *New York Post*.

His children, fairly composed, occassionally whispered to him, and Simpson unashamedly and guiltlessly embraced Nicole's family members.

Among the mourners were O.J.'s friends and supporters Al Cowlings, Bob Chandler, former Olympic star Bruce Jenner, and Steve Garvey.

Sydney, Nicole and O.J.'s eight-year-old daughter, seemed to be on the verge of tears by the close of the funeral ceremony. Justin, five, looked confused and kept seeking reassurance, gazing up at his father's face, puzzled by the emotion that was etched there, and the anguish of his older sister, his grandparents and his acquaintances.

Meanwhile, Ronald Lyle Goldman's funeral was held in Agoura Hills, California, at the Valley Oaks Cemetery. Goldman was buried in a plot under a spreading Oregon pine tree.

A crowd of four hundred friends and relatives—and 23 camera crews—attended the event. Rabbi Gary Johnson of Temple Beth Haverim read a poem about love that Goldman had written to a girlfriend in the past, when he lived in the middle-class suburbs of Agoura Hills, and not in the posh region around Brentwood.

Goldman's sister, Pam, shared a message with the mourners.

"Thank you for being my brother," she said. "I love you."

One mourner characterized Ronald Goldman as a "forgotten victim."

At this point, some members of the press suddenly changed their early characterization of Goldman. In the very beginning, after the first reports about Goldman and Nicole Brown Simpson emerged, the press hinted at a romantic involvement between the older woman and the younger man.

By Thursday, the tone of these reports changed. Overnight, television and print journalists were calling him an innocent bystander who rushed to help Nicole when she was attacked and was then murdered for his rash but very heroic act.

The police refused to comment on the time of deaths, or whether the victims were murdered at the same time or a few minutes apart, and so this characterization of the incidents and Goldman's real reason for being at the Simpson townhouse are still questionable.

Was he just there to return the glasses, or was there something more to his presence at Nicole Simpson's townhouse that evening?

Los Angeles detectives flew to Chicago to help local authorities investigate the hotel room where Simpson stayed for an hour and a half on Monday morning.

The LAPD's office kept insisting that an "arrest was imminent," and it was apparent that—after being stung by the inability to get a guilty verdict in the highly-publicized Menendez murders, their failure to charge Michael Jackson for child molestation, and their inability to get a guilty verdict against the officers who beat Rodney King—the Los An-

geles District Attorney's office was working
on building a rock-solid case against O.J.
Simpson.

Reports first surfaced at this time about
the eight different times police were called
to the Simpson home by Nicole to protect
her from her husband—which only resulted
in one arrest. This caused a furor of further
criticism of both the LAPD and the DA's office. Later on, District Attorney Gil Garcetti
would concede that the sentencing Simpson
received after his 1989 assault of Nicole was
"absurd." Of course, it happened before
Garcetti was in charge, and made domestic
violence something of a crusade.

The police leaks indicated that bits of flesh
were indeed found under the fingernails of one
or both of the victims. This story, reported on
a Los Angeles television news show the day
before, was still not verified by police.

In Chicago, acting on a tip, Chicago police
and Los Angeles detectives searched a vacant
and overgrown lot near the O'Hare Plaza-Hotel for the murder weapon. They used metal
detectors and a battery of officers to search
the area.

They found nothing, and are still searching for the murder weapon as of this writing.

Simpson's lawyer hires a lab crime sleuth, Dr. Henry Lee, head of the Connecticut State Police forensics lab, and Michael Baden, the New York State medical examiner who served on the Warren Commission investigation into the assassination of John F. Kennedy.

Baden and Lee were hired to evaluate the evidence against Simpson for the defense. Lee's last high-profile case was as part of the defense team in the William Kennedy Smith rape trial in Palm Beach. Reconstructing crimes is one of his specialties.

Simpson's alibi that he was home alone at the time of the killings had still not changed, despite the challenge to that testimony offered by the limo driver.

Even without that challenge, the Los Angeles detectives working the case felt that Simpson had more than enough time to murder his ex-wife and Goldman, drive the paltry two miles to his house, jump into the limo (after a shower?) and make it to LAX in time for his flight to Chicago.

Bolstered by the battery of forensic test results, the police decided they could now ar-

rest Simpson and set that event into motion.
They phoned Simpson's lawyer and arranged
a time for his surrender to authorities.

Shapiro consulted with his high-profile client
and a time was arranged—Simpson would surrender to police at 11:00 a.m., PDT the next day.

It seems, after the events of Friday have unfolded, that Simpson himself had another plan
in mind. In a desperate scheme, Simpson
planned to escape the ranks of press and television crews camped out in front of his Brentwood
estate, and made arrangements of his own.

O.J. accepted an invitation offered by his
friend Robert Kardashian, to stay at Kardashian's private home in the San Fernando Valley. He never told police about these
arrangements, and it is still unclear at the time
of this writing how he left the Brentwood mansion without the press—or the police—seeing
him.

The end, it seemed, was near . . .

FRIDAY, JUNE 17

The strangest day since the night of the
terrible murders that rocked America was beginning.

As 11:00 a.m., PDT approached, Simpson and his long-time friend Al Cowlings, sat alone in a room on the ground floor of Kardashian's house. Simpson's lawyer, Robert Shapiro, had just given the superstar sixty dollars in cash so that he would have some money for the jail commisary.

It must have been at that frozen moment that O.J. Simpson realized he was going to jail—possibly forever. He no doubt felt trapped, with no way out. Tortured either by a guilty conscience or the hounding of the press and the stains covering his long-standing reputation, he decided to bolt. Doctors, called on the scene by Shapiro, had informed both O.J. and his lawyer that they had, upon examination, found strange lumps under his armpits—his lymph nodes were swollen. This might indicate that he was suffering from an infection, but one physician thought that it might be more serious. O.J. Simpson might have cancer, the doctor said. As Shapiro spoke with the physicians on the second-floor of the Kardashian residence, Simpson and Cowlings rushed out to Cowlings' white Bronco and sped away—leaving a shocked and disturbed Robert Shapiro embarrassed and humiliated by his celebrity client.

Though it was not public knowledge yet, O.J. Simpson was now a fugitive from justice.

The Los Angeles Police Depart announced a press conference that would, as was speculated by journalists, publically announce that charges were filed against O.J. Simpson for double-murder. After a long delay—and a phoned in bomb threat that forced the authorities to clear the room of the press and abandon the building—the press conference was finally held over a hour late.

Commander David Gascon announced that after an exhaustive investigation and an extensive examination of the physical evidence, the police sought and obtained a warrant for Simpson's arrest.

Gascon told the packed-newsroom that he and his lawyer were supposed to surrender the gridiron legend at 11:00 a.m.—then at 11:30. When Simpson did not appear after those deadlines passed, the police confessed to the press—in yet another stunning bombshell—that O.J. was a fugitive from justice.

The members of the press present were visibly shocked by the news.

An angry and frustrated Los Angeles District Attorney, Gil Garcetti, in a subsequent press conference, announced that charges of

First Degree Murder with Special Circumstances were filed against Simpson, and
warned anyone who was helping him that
they would face felony charges and could
also face a still prison term.

The police told the press and a surprised
world that the former football legend was
presumed to be "armed, dangerous and sui-
cidal."

At that point, said Gil Garcetti, the Simp-
son/Goldman murder case was entering the
prosecutorial stage.

A manhunt ensued. Police were sent to
watch the Mexican border and the airports
and train stations.

Meanwhile, Robert Kardashian read one of
three letters written by O.J. Simpson (see Ap-
pendix) to his public. The other two letters
were addressed to his children from both
marriages and his mother, Eunice. The letter
addressed to the public was read by Robert
Kardashian to reporters at a press conference. The former gridiron star said "I can't
go on," and begged the press to leave his
innocent children alone. He added that he
hoped that people would remember him as
he once was—a football star on top of the
world, and not "this lost person."

In the letter he reiterated his innocence, and poignantly spoke of his troubled but loving relationship with Nicole. He also spoke fondly of his friends, men like Al Cowlings and Wayne Hughes, Louis Marx and Bobby Kardashian, Bob Chandler and Ahmad Rashad, the former athlete turned sports broadcaster for NBC.

He also thanked his first wife, Marguerite, and Paula Barbieri, the devout Christian model he was recently dating.

Police psychologists and other experts all shared the opinion that this was a suicide note.

The manhunt that was launched was a mercifully short one.

At around 7:00 p.m. PDT, the police received a phone call from Al Cowlings stating that he was in his Ford Bronco, driving down highway five.

Cowlings told the press that everything was fine at that moment, but that O.J. had a gun to his head and would blow his own brains out if anybody tried to stop the car or block the roadway.

The Larry King Show, on CNN, as well as the NBA playoffs viewed by millions, were suddenly interrupted by live coverage of the low-speed chase that was taking place on the highways of Los Angeles at that same time.

Inside a white Ford Bronco, O.J. Simpson, a gun to his head, was being driven to see his mother by Al Cowlings, his childhood friend and fellow teammate at junior college, USC, and the Buffalo Bills.

Simpson, it was later learned, was traced through cellular phone calls he and Cowlings placed to various locations—including, it is rumored, Nicole's Brentwood townhouse, where her father frantically phoned 911 after Simpson called and stated he was on his way there.

Was Simpson attempting to flee? If so, where could such a public persona go to hide?

Psychologists speak about the patterns that men who kill their spouses usually follow— and if Simpson *did* kill his wife, was he following one of these recognizable patterns? Was O.J. Simpson, like Shakespeare's Othello, going to his ex-wife's home, or her grave, to commit suicide?

Or was he an innocent man driven to the edge of madness by hounding police and the reporters who gathered like hyenas to feed

on the carrion of his fallen life, his fallen
reputation?

As millions watched, Simpson and Cowlings drove slowly along various Los Angeles
freeways, dodging traffic when the police
had not managed to clear the highway. It was
stated on television that O.J. was heading to
his Brentwood home, and thousands of his
fans and curiosity seekers lined the highway,
some cheering the former gridiron star on
with shouts of "Go, Juice, go!" and "Juice!
Juice! Juice!"

The Bronco, with cameras focused on it
from helicopters overhead, turned down Sun-
set Boulevard and headed toward the
Brentwood mansion. Cowlings stated over the
car phone, over and over again, that O.J. just
wanted to see his mother, Eunice.

Word of the flight, broadcast on a hundred televisions and watched by millions of
viewers in the Los Angeles area, spread like
wildfire in the dry winds of Southern California. Crowds of people, recognizing the
road and the direction of the Bronco's path,
rushed to the roadway, the overpasses, and
cheered the fugitive on. Other cars on the
freeway pulled over to the side of the road.

Some drivers, spotting O.J. Simpson, used their own cellular phones to report that he was rushing down the freeway.

One call reported that O.J. "stared us down . . . he gave us a look like death, man."

The Bronco cruised along the San Diego Freeway, and people began to push lawnchairs to the edge of the freeway, waiting for the show to pass them by. Some held signs that read "Go, O.J. Go" All were shouting and calling to the car as it passed them.

The rest of America was riveted to their television sets, the NBA finals forgotten. Even sports journalists at the New York game rushed to nearby television monitors and their broadcast booths to watch the chase in Los Angeles. Basketball was forgotten, the real drama was happening on a California freeway thousands of miles away.

Downtown, as Los Angeles police headquarters, Special Weapons and Tactics Teams—SWAT teams—were being readied for any eventuality. Crisis negotiators were also being notified and they watched the televisions and monitored the radio as they rushed to the superstar's presumed destination—his Brentwood home.

The twenty-five man SWAT team was dispatched to the Brentwood mansion in unmarked cars. They split into teams, and snipers were stationed on roofs in case the unthinkable happened. Some wondered if Cowlings was a hostage—though he himself kept denying it. The cops fanned out into the bushes and behind the palm trees that lined the street around Simpson's home.

The crowds waiting in vigil around Simpson's home hampered their efforts. Days before the police began issuing tickets to parked cars in the area, and even arresting "vagrants"—but nothing could deter his many fans, who just kept coming, or merely driving past.

Now they were clearly in the way and the cops were angry.

Fortunately, Simpson and Cowlings chose to turn into a back entrance, eluding the bulk of the crowds.

With police and press helicopters overhead, and a host of police units following behind, the Bronco was allowed to enter the Brentwood compound.

Simpson's son Jason, when he saw his besieged father in the car, broke free of the police in the mansion's doorway and ran toward the car.

"Who the hell is that?"

"That's his son" shouted one of the cops on the scene, clearly concerned for the boy's safety.

"Get him the hell out of there," another screamed as the weeping young man confronted Cowlings, who was crying as well. Two uniformed policemen calmly approached the car and dragged the crying youth back into the house.

The SWAT team was weighing its choices— should they use tear gas, or charge the car in hope of a desperately quick save? Snipers were also an option.

Cowlings refused to abandon O.J., his life-long pal.

No one wanted to kill O.J. Simpson on live television.

After a delay in which police negotiators talked to O.J., both over the car phone and from across the driveway, the superstar was permitted to enter his house and presumably speak to his mother over the phone.

Police reportedly had instructions to "take him out" had Simpson not surrendered promptly, but officers later stated that killing him was never an option unless he fired at them or someone else first.

The dramatic, daylong manhunt came to an end when a distraught Simpson dropped his blue steel revolver and exited the Bronco. He was clutching family pictures of himself, Nicole and the children. He was crying and said to one of the arresting officers, "I'm sorry I made you do this."

Several minutes later, O.J. Simpson surrendered to the police and was taken to police headquarters for fingerprinting and mug shots.

Later that evening, Eunice Simpson, O.J.'s 72-year old mother, was admitted to the California Pacific Medical Center in San Francisco after suffering from the stress of watching her son's desperate chase and arrest.

The Los Angeles Police came under widespread criticism when it was discovered that there was no twenty-four hour watch on the Simpson home, nor, as D.A. Gil Garcetti conceded, did the police know his exact whereabouts at the time of his scheduled surrender. They did not know he was at the Kardashian house, nor that he skipped out with Cowlings until much later.

Robert Shapiro was criticized, and he was

also humiliated by his client's behavior. He accepted O.J.'s apologies and continues to represent him.

Again, the press concluded, the LAPD had dropped the ball.

Simpson was placed in a cell, and put under a twenty-four hour suicide watch.

A suicide watch is a complicated affair, and quite labor intensive. Prison guards and officials must constantly watch the prisoner—checking the cell every fifteen minutes, twenty-four hours a day. Some facilities speak to the prisoner at each fifteen-minute interval, night and day, waking them often throughout the night. Other facilities are more relaxed, but not much more relaxed. The prisoner must eat in his cell, with plastic utensils that must be accounted for after the meal.

A television may be brought in for only a few hours each day. No sheets or towels are issued to someone on a suicide watch—so that they cannot tie them together and make a noose. Some prison officials speak of flimsy clothes issued to the inmate, so that if they tie these clothes together, the fiber is too weak to support their weight. They are, of course, not issued belts, or even ties on the pants.

Often the cell itself is specially-designed, with no light sockets or fixtures on the ceiling which can be used to tie a rope. In some more modern facilities, the toilet in the cell does not fill with water, and is built on a much smaller scale, so that the prisoner cannot stick his or her head into it and drown themselves.

Shaving is not permitted, except in the presence of a prison guard. The prisoner on suicide watch is only permitted to shower every other day. There is no privacy whatsoever on a suicide watch.

MONDAY, JUNE 19

A chronology of events on the day of the murders began to emerge on Monday

Mostly the information dealt with the events directly preceeding the crimes, at the recital attended by Nicole Brown Simpson, her two children Justin and Sydney, and O.J. Simpson himself. This new information shed much light on those events and the state of mind the former football star was in. It is a harrowing picture of a man on the edge, a woman frightened by and for the man she once loved, and the final tragedy of murder.

It was another beautiful afternoon—the kind that only happened in Southern California. Four miles dead east of posh, celebrity-paced Beverly Hills lay the equally posh suburb of Brentwood.

As a hundred or more luxury cars—a car thieves dreamland—packed the parking lot of the Paul Revere School, parents and children filed into the auditorium for a dance recital that had been scheduled for weeks.

The theme of the recital was the Old West. The parents of these very affluent children spared no expense and the youngsters were all dressed in expensive leather and gingham. There were sheriffs, gunfighters, cowboys and cowgirls, saloon dancers and even the occasional cattle-rustler. The scene was loud and happy, with children calling out across the room to their friends, and parents greeting their fellow tony neighbors, exchanging gossip and talking about the next big deal they, or their husbands or wives, were working on. All the better to stay ahead, and keep the luxurious lifestyle that took plenty of work to maintain.

Then the lights dimmed and the recital began, the music filled the auditorium. The first act filed out onto the stage and the show began.

As the recital commenced, O.J. Simpson, according to reports on *A Current Affair*, approached his ex-wife and spoke to her as she watched the first act begin to dance. O.J. reportedly asked Nicole if he could sit with her. She apparently refused. According to various reports that have recently come to light, Nicole felt threatened by her ex-husband. He was arriving at her condominum at all hours, unannounced, and she was tired of her privacy being invaded by the man that was the father of her children—but whom she was divorced from. Nicole wanted to get on with her life, and was even dating several men, one of them she may have been serious about.

There were reportedly no harsh words said, but Nicole's refusal was adamant. She did not want to sit with her ex-husband.

The recital continued, and O.J. sat a row, or several rows behind her (accounts differ). One little girl dancing her heart out was Sydney Simpson, and she did her number wearing a toy six-shooter and singing "Oklahoma" with the other children. One report stated that she had a solo dance number to the tune of *Footloose*.

All the parents were proud of their little

ones, and all eyes, and several video cameras, followed the children through their tap-dancing and square dancing routines. The recital was a long one, and the room heated up, but the parents stuck it out, waiting for their own child's moment of glory and fame.

As the recital ended and the parents sent their kids and the other children who participated a standing ovation. Nicole gathered her children to her and, with friends and family—including Nicole's two sisters—they headed to her rented limo.

"It was just a great, happy, silly end to the school year.

"Everybody was smiling. Cameras were clicking left and right," one member of the audience recalled.

Another parent told of the many video cameras in the room—these were affluent parents, after all, and it was their little darlings up on that stage.

At about 4:30 p.m. PDT, O.J. Simpson approached Nicole once more and asked if he could go to dinner with her and the children and their friends and family. Nicole again refused.

No doubt, we can surmise, the fear that she expressed to Dr. Susan Forward, the fear of O.J.'s seemingly obsessive behavior toward her, effected her feelings toward her ex-husband. She was probably tired of his many attempts at reconciliation, weary of his constant attentions. She probably felt that the abuse that he sometimes dealt her—at least on that one occasion on New Year's 1989—had finally beat all the love she had for this man out of her. She did not want to encourage him further.

It was the wise thing, but it no doubt left O.J. feeling dejected and rejected. Did that moment in time finally harden his heart? Was that the moment of decision? Or did Simpson simply leave, head home, pack for his trip and depart for the airport, as the ex-gridiron star maintains? That is for a jury to decide.

At any case, when Nicole refused his request to join her and the children at Mezzaluna, O.J. took his two kids in his arms and said good-bye. He made of point of telling them that he was heading out to Chicago, and that they could reach him there if they needed him for anything—there was never any doubt that O.J. Simpson loved his children, and Nicole.

A short time after five that afternoon, the party of ten arrived at Mezzaluna. Ronald Goldman, familiar with the stunning blond and her children, was said by one account to wave to them from across the room. He worked at Mezzaluna as a waiter, but he was not their waiter that night.

Goldman has been described as one of Nicole's "best friends" and was said to be a bodybuilder who had modeled for Giorgio Armani apparel, and had quite a reputation as a ladies man. This reputation was borne out by the number of very pretty young women who turned out for the young man's funeral.

"A real romantic guy," the *New York Post* called him.

But "To a point." the *Post* added. "What Ronald Goldman really liked to do was see a maximum number of women in the minimum amount of time.

"And he was the love-'em-and-leave-'em type who didn't mind bragging about his conquests."

Ronald Lyle Goldman—who had once appeared on the tacky Fox television show *Studs*, a show in which several "hunks" vie for the attentions of a "babe" or "babes" and then they date, return to the studio and talk about it—was very vain and very ambitious. The show was total sleeze, with a capital "S," but no doubt Goldman believed it would forward his careers as both a model and an actor.

Nicole, Justin, Sydney, her parents, and Nicole's two sisters, and three other friends sat down to their long table in the crowded and popular upscale restaurant. Suddenly, Goldman walked over to the crowded table where Nicole sat and kneeled down between her and the kids. "It was a cozy scene with the kids squealing, 'Ron! Ron!'" reported the *New York Post* on Tuedsay, June 21.

This brief but telling display of familiarity and affection left no question in many people's minds that Nicole did know Goldman, and knew him quite well. Other reports have surfaced that link Goldman with Nicole, reports that even indicated that Simpson had met the twenty-five-year-old Goldman and even spent time with him.

There were stories that he was seen in Brentwood, driving Nicole's white Ferrari, both with the beautiful blond and her children, and alone. Few reports, however, linked them romantically—in fact, there may have *been* a romantic interest in Nicole's life at that time, but it seems clear now that, at least by the Spring of 1994, Goldman was not Nicole's lover.

They were probably familiar with each other because they both worked out at the same health club—"The Gym"—and as their friendship grew, Goldman often stopped by Nicole's condo, which was only a few blocks from Mezzaluna. It has been reported that Nicole accompanied Goldman to a model shoot, though at that time no one knew who she was. The assumption, according to the photographer at the shoot, was that she was Goldman's "meal ticket."

At one time, according to a *Hard Copy* report, when a friend of Goldman's asked him point blank if he was sleeping with Nicole, the model-turned-waiter, replied that if he did, "O.J. would kill me."

According to the *New York Post*, Goldman was once quizzed by a neighbor about what O.J. Simpson would think if he saw him at the wheel of the car O.J. once owned, the white Ferrari convertible that Nicole got through the divorce settlement. The young model was said to shudder and then stated, "I think he'd wanna kill me."

At any case, Ronald Goldman returned to his duties as a waiter for the opposite side of the room, and the dinner party continued, with much laughter and good cheer. As the meal ended, Sydney and Justin looked tired, so Nicole said her good-byes and they were on their way. Nicole was probably tired, too, and she tucked her little ones into bed at around 9:00 PDT.

It was probably only a short time after that when Nicole realized she had left her expensive sunglasses behind at the restaurant. She called the trendy restaurant to inquire about them. They had indeed been discovered, the manager replied, and offered to hold them for her or take them over himself, as he was just ready to drive home.

The manager, according to reports on both *Hard Copy* and *A Current Affair*, was then interrupted by Goldman, who suggested that he could take the glasses over himself, as he was set to get off work at 9:30. The manager told *Hard Copy* that he offered to drive Goldman over to the Simpson house, but Goldman replied that it was a nice night, and he would walk, or something to that effect.

At between 9:40 and 10:00 p.m., PDT, Ronale Lyle Goldman reached the home of Nicole Brown Simpson. She invited him in for a short time. The children, by that time, were asleep.

Within the next forty-five minutes, the relentless barking of one—and possibly two—dogs shattered the more predictable sounds of crickets chirping and cool Southern California breezes rustling the palm trees.

According to the *New York Post* and the *Los*

Angeles Times, neighbors later told police that they first heard the dog—or dogs—barking, and then other loud noises.

The *Post* account states that "One nearby resident described what sounded like blood-curdling screams."

If there were screams—and as of this writing that fact has not been verified and other newspaper reports make no mention of it—then those screams were, according to the *Post*, the "tortured cries of help from Nicole and Goldman as someone surprised them with a 'large knife' as they walked onto the front porch of the condo."

It is apparent that Goldman did not stay long—there was no tryst—because no one entered Nicole Simpson's house. The bodies were later discovered outside of the townhouse, on the tiled sidewalk, Nicole lying on her side, Goldman face down. The tiles, the walls around the walkway, and the nearby shrubbery were splattered with the victims' blood.

Goldman—a bodybuilder, a big man described as possessing "large, rippling muscles," put up a fierce struggle. Were the "fragments of flesh" that the Los Angeles Medical Examiners' Office were later to subject to various DNA tests found under the carefully manicured fingers of Ronald Lyle Goldman? As yet the police have not responded to that question.

In any case, the knife wounds, the savagery of the attack, the merciless way in which the wounds were inflicted indicate that the attack was fast, and strong, and overpowered the struggling Goldman. The attacker had to be a large man, too, a man physically fit and trained in agression.

This, again, begs the question. Was the attacker an athlete?

According to a reconstruction of the events of the crime, Goldman dropped to the ground, and it was then that the attacker finished the deadly act of cutting his throat, from-ear-to-ear in the popular parlance. Nicole, then, or perhaps before, suffered a similar and terrible fate. What the police now know is that the killings occurred between 9:45 and 11:00 p.m. PDT.

O.J. Simpson's home is just two miles away, and if he indeed committed these two horrible crimes, then the superstar had plenty of time to get back to his own home, change, and get ready for his trip. Yet, according to the limo driver dispatched to bring O.J. to the airport, he was not at his residence at 11:00, when the driver arrived.

If he did commit those terrible murders, what did O.J. do in the ensuing hour, when a five minute trip would have taken him to his home?

Reports surfacing Monday, June 20 suggest that there may have been an accomplice to the crime. The grand jury, which convened to decide whether or not to charge the former football star and commercial spokesman, leaked to the press that there was another party involved, a party that refused to testify to that grand jury unless promised immunity from prosecution.

Who was this mysterious witness, or accomplice? As of Tuesday, June 22, he was identified as "Kato" Kaelin, who lived in O.J. Simpson's guest house and was at the mansion the night the NFL Hall-of-Famer allegedly killed his ex-wife and her friend. According to the New York *Daily News*, Kaelin debunked Simpson's claim that he was home at the time of the murders.

In any case, the sound of barking ceased, the crickets resumed their song, and quiet once again reigned in Brentwood, on Bundy Drive. That quiet was not to last long, on this winding and shaded street that was intersected by busier boulevards with more familiar names, and just across the invisible border from Santa Monica.

A scream shattered the peace this time, as a woman walking her dog saw a river of red running down the sidewalk. When she went to investigate, she saw the grisly sight of the slashed bodies, the splattered blood on the sidewalk and the walls. What little peace remained at that point was soon broken forever.

The neighborhood was roused by the sounds of sirens as a dozen or more police cars converged on the scene from both directions. People from the surrounding residences rushed to their windows, their doors, out onto the street in their casual nightclothes. It was murder, someone said. A collective shudder went through the neighborhood as the police surrounded the area with the yellow ribbons marked "Police Line Do Not Cross."

The cops, it was revealed on Monday, June 20, knew immediately who the female victim was. As they entered the house and found the two sleeping children—who had mercifully missed the carnage—a black-and-white squad car was sent to the Simpson residence to tell the beloved football star the tragic and terrible news. He was not at home.

As the police forensic experts arrived, the officers took blood samples, crime photos, and wiped up the blood surrounding the corpses with towels. The experts could then approach the victims and get hair and flesh samples from under the fingernails of one—or both—of them. The news began to reach the media at this time.

This was the story that hit the newsstands and the television airwaves on Monday, June 20 and Tuesday, June 21.

It is only a reconstruction of events, and the facts may change with time and further investigation—including DNA testing (which can take weeks or even months), hair and fiber tests, the grilling of more witnesses like the jogger who claimed to see O.J. Simpson's own white Bronco—much like the one that belonged to his best friend Al Cowlings—at the Nicole Simpson residence that evening at around 10:00 p.m. And, of course, the unnamed mystery witness who demands immunity from prosecution before he or she will talk about the crime to authorities.

At 12:00 noon, PDT, Simpson appeared at his arraignment.

O.J. Simpson was formally charged with First Degree Murder. He pleaded not guilty. Simpson was obviously bleary eyed during this process, and he seemed almost disoriented and confused. He did, however, answer all of the judge's questions and stated that he understood the charges being made against him.

During the course of this process, Robert Shapiro kept his right hand on O.J. Simpson's shoulder and whispered advice and counseling into the much-taller athlete's ear.

As of this writing, Simpson's hearing is scheduled for June 30, 1994, at 9:30 a.m. PDT. Shapiro, the dealmaker and brilliant attorney, is now playing hardball, and demanding a speedy trial.

TUESDAY, JUNE 21

Loose talk is beginning to emerge about O.J.'s eventual defense, should the case ever go to trial.

There is talk in the press of the "steroid insanity plea."

It was Cindy Adams who first published this story, in her column for June 21.

"O.J.'s defense will be naturally, insanity," she wrote.

"The buzz is, insanity by reason of steroids. Since he hasn't been a working athlete in years and, thus, would probably not have taken steroids recently, if ever, I don't quite know what this means.

"But I'm repeating what I'm told."

The story also emerged on the Tuesday following the arrest that the Los Angeles DA could possibly let Al Cowlings off the hook.

Cowlings, who was freed on $250,000 bond, may actually escape prosecution because of the very public outpouring of support the man—who was only trying to help his best friend in the world—has received.

Cowlings "risked his own life to save his pal," said Darrell Ruocco, a former roomate of Cowlings.

"Obviously, he is an incredible person."

But L.A. District Attorney Gil Garcetti says the charges will be dropped only if it can be established that Cowlings was acting under duress when he drove Simpson through Los Angeles on that final flight.

Cowlings' lawyer, Donald Re—a former partner of Howard Weitzman—remains, as of this writing, unavailable for comment.

If your best friend came to you for help, what would you do?

What would you do?

* * *

Reports also began to emerge about Simpson's erratic behavior before the murder.

According to a report in the *New York Post*, the superstar exploded into a terrible rage when he was playing golf with his friends on the day of the murders.

Michael Mesko, a caddie at the exclusive Riviera Country Club, told the press and the television show *A Current Affair* that he was caddying for O. J. Simpson and some of his pals when Simpson became violent and explosive.

Mesko relates that a motion picture producer named Craig Baumgarten had just teed off with a terrible shot and he teasingly blamed O.J. for the bad drive. Instead of laughing at the jibe, the superstar let loose with a stream of invectives.

"Why are you blaming this on me?

"Everytime your goddamn shit gets funky, you want to blame it on me or someone else."

O.J. then threatened the producer with physical violence.

"I will kick your ass right here on this mother fuckin' golf course if you say one more word."

Everyone in the golf party was quite shocked by this uncharacteristic outburst. Masko told the tabloid journalism show that Baumgarten and O.J. had made up by the end of the game, but "things suddenly turned maudlin," the *New York Post* reported.

Simpson, after the outburst, turned to his caddy and said, "Mitch, I'm a pathetic person."

Mesko was reported to be "shocked" by the legend's statement and he told O.J.:

" 'Juice', you're not a pathetic person . . . You're a pathetic golfer."

Simpson laughed then, and told Mesko, "I'll remember that remark, I am a pathetic golfer."

This was about twelve hours before the murders.

Allegations of cocaine and crack cocaine use by Simpson also surfaced on Tuesday, June 12.

It was longtime friend, and longtime rival Jim Brown who made the charges. Although the allegations are scathing, and very damaging to the former All-American's reputation, Brown offered no proof. The charges were made on the ABC television show, *Good Morning America*.

"The truth shall prevail," Brown said. "Of course there were problems with drugs with O.J. Why shouldn't I say it now?"

Brown said he was saddened watching Simpson being chased by police on that fateful Friday, and saddened to see him in police custody. He told the nation that "I really think it's a point of not recognizing someone fully who is suffering because of the whole emphasis on money and celebrity."

When Brown was asked why he didn't intervene to help Simpson if he believed that the man was suffering from an addiction, Brown stated that:

"I wasn't that kind of friend . . .

"O.J. was living a different life than I live, O.J. was in the elite circles . . . He was a person that understood how to use the system properly."

Brown said Simpson often bragged about the amount of money he was making, and his ability to make more.

"(Simpson) knew that in order to make the money and to be the darling of America, he had to present himself a certain way . . . He had to be approved of. And when you have to be approved of, it's never going to be real.

"Because the people approving of you are not interested in you. They are interested in you as a product and what you can produce."

There are a battery of legal steps to be taken in the case of O.J. Simpson and the murder of Nicole Brown Simpson and Ronald Lyle Goldman.

These steps are as follows:

THE COMPLIANCE HEARING (Scheduled, as of this writing, for June 22, 1994)

This hearing will determine if the coroner complied with a request by Simpson's attorney to gain access to all autopsy information.

Here the judge will also determine whether officials turned over to Simpson's defense team all the relevant police information on the slayings. This includes reports, eyewitness accounts, time of death, etc.

THE PRELIMINARY HEARING (Scheduled for June 30, 1994 as of this writing)

At this hearing prosecutors must show that the case should go to trial.

If the judge determines that there is sufficient evidence to go to trial, then the case will be bound over to Superior Court and at that time a trial judge will be assigned.

If the prosecution fails to convince the judge that there is enough evidence to prosecute, then the case could be dismissed at this stage. The circumstantial evidence, according to legal experts, is sufficient already to bound O.J. Simpson over to trial in California.

THE GRAND JURY

At any time in the process, a grand jury could issue an indictment and the grand jury in the Simpson case has already begun hearing that testimony. They have already spoken to a number of witnesses and it was at this stage of the trial phase—which began almost immediately after the crime was committed—that the grand jury spoke to the unidentified witness who is demanding immunity from prosecution.

If—or when—the grand jury issues their indictment, the case will then go straight to Superior Court to be tried with a jury.

Murder in the First Degree, with Special Circumstances, is a capital charge in California. If convicted of all charges, O.J. Simpson could face the death penalty. In that circumstance, O.J. would have a choice of death by lethal injection, or the gas chamber.

There are 383 death row prisoners in California. Men awaiting execution in California are kept at the prison called San Quentin.

Twelve

TRANSCRIPT OF NICOLE'S CALL TO 911

On June 23 the LAPD released a dramatic tape of Nicole Simpson's tearful call to 911 on October 25, 1993. The tape was made after a furious O.J. had kicked in the back door of Nicole's home, because he had seen a picture of an ex-boyfriend in her photo album.

The voice of O.J. Simpson can be heard in the background, shouting obscenities as the trembling voice of Nicole speaks to the 911 operator. At the very least, the tape gives credence to rumors that the 1989 incident was not an isolated one.

NICOLE: My ex-husband has just broken into my house and he's ranting and raving outside in the front yard.
911: Has he been drinking or anything?

NICOLE: No. But he's crazy.
911: Did he hit you?
NICOLE: No.
911: Do you have a restraining order against him?
NICOLE: No.
911: What is your name?
NICOLE: Nicole Simpson.

NICOLE: Could you get somebody over here now, to . . . Gretna Green. He's back. Please.
911: What does he look like?
NICOLE: He's O.J. Simpson. I think you know his record. Could you just send somebody over here?
911: What is he doing there?
NICOLE: He just drove up again. [Nicole begins to cry.] Could you just send somebody over?
911: What is he driving?
NICOLE: He's in a white Bronco, but first of all he broke the back door down to get in.
911: Wait a minute, what's your name?
NICOLE: Nicole Simpson.
911: OK, is he sportscaster or whatever?
NICOLE: Yeah.
911: Wait a minute, we're sending police. What is he doing? Is he threatening you?
NICOLE: He's f——g going nuts. [She can be heard sobbing.]
911: Has he threatened you or is he just harassing you?

NICOLE: You're going to hear him in a minute. He's about to come in again.

911: OK, just stay on the line.

NICOLE: I don't want to stay on the line. He's going to beat the s— out of me.

911: Wait a minute, just stay on the line so we can know what's going on until the police get here, OK? OK Nicole?

NICOLE: Uh-huh.

911: Just a moment. Does he have any weapons?

NICOLE: I don't know. [She sighs.] He went home. Now he's back. The kids are up there sleeping and I don't want anything to happen.

911: OK, just a minute. Is he on drugs or anything?

NICOLE: No.

911: Just stay on the line. In case he comes in I need to hear what's going on.

NICOLE: Can you hear him outside?

911: Is he yelling?

NICOLE: Yep.

911: OK. Has he been drinking?

NICOLE: No.

911: OK. [Can be heard contacting police units.] All units: more on the domestic violence at . . . South Gretna Green Way, the suspect has returned in a white Bronco. Monitor comments. Incident 48231.

[The operator then returns her attention to Nicole.]

OK, Nicole?

NICOLE: Uh-huh.

911: Is he outdoors?

NICOLE: Uh-huh, he's in the back yard.

911: He's in the back yard?

NICOLE: Screaming at my roommate about me and at me.

911: OK. What is he saying?

NICOLE: Oh, something about a guy I know and hookers and keys and I started this s— before and—

911: Um-hum.

NICOLE: And it's all my fault and 'Now what am I going to do,' 'get the police in this' and the whole thing. It's all my fault, I started this before. [Sigh.] Brother . . . [inaudible] kids . . . [inaudible].

911: OK, has he hit you today or . . .

NICOLE: No.

911: OK, you don't need any paramedics or anything. OK, you just want him to leave?

NICOLE: My door. He broke the whole back door in.

911: And then he left and he came back?

NICOLE: He came and he practically knocked my upstairs door down but he pounded it and he screamed and hollered and I tried to get him out of the bedroom because the kids are sleeping there.

911: Um-hum. OK.

NICOLE: He wanted somebody's phone number and I gave him my phone book or I put my phone book down to write down the phone number that he wanted and he took my phone book with all my stuff in it.

911: OK. So basically you guys have just been arguing?

[O.J. continues yelling in the background.]

911: Is he inside right now?
NICOLE: Yeah.

[O.J. is still yelling.]

911: Is he talking to you?
NICOLE: Yeah.
911: Are you locked in a room or something?
NICOLE: No. He can come right in. I'm not going
where the kids are because the kids . . .
911: Do you think he's going to hit you?
NICOLE: I don't know.
911: Stay on the line. Don't hang it up, OK?
NICOLE: OK.

[Tape is inaudible at this point.]

911: What is he saying?
[Sound of police radio in the background.]
NICOLE: O.J. O.J. The kids are sleeping.

[O.J. continues to yell.]

911: He's still yelling at you?

[Sound of screaming. Nicole sobs into the tele-
phone.]

911: Is he upset with something that you did?
NICOLE: [Sobs.] A long time ago. It always comes
back.
911: Is your roommate talking to him?
NICOLE: No one can talk, listen to him.

911: Does he have any weapons with him right now?

NICOLE: No, uh-uh.

911: OK. Where is he standing?

NICOLE: In the back doorway, in the house.

911: OK.

O.J.: . . . I don't give a s— anymore . . ."

NICOLE: Would you please, O.J. O.J., O.J., O.J., could you please [*inaudible*], please leave.

O.J.: . . . I'm not leaving . . .

NICOLE: Please leave, O.J. Please, the kids, the kids are sleeping, please.

911: Is he leaving?

NICOLE: No.

911: Does he know you're on the phone with police?

NICOLE: No.

911: Where are the kids right now?

NICOLE: Up in my room.

911: Can they hear him yelling?

NICOLE: I don't know. The room's the only one that's quiet . . . God.

911: Is there someone up there with the kids?

NICOLE: No.

[The sound of O.J. yelling can still be heard in the background.]

911: What is he saying now? Nicole, you still on the line?

NICOLE: Yeah.

911: Do you still think he's going to hit you?

NICOLE: I don't know. He's going to leave. He just said that, he just said he needs to leave.

O.J.: . . . Hey! I can read this bulls— all week in the

National Enquirer. Her words exactly. What, who got that, who? . . .
911: Are you the only in there with him?
NICOLE: Right now, yeah. And he's also talking to my, the guy who lives out back is just standing there. He came home.
911: Are you arguing with him, too?
NICOLE: No. Absolutely not.
911: Oh, OK. OK.
NICOLE: That's not arguing.
911: Yeah. Has this happened before or no?
NICOLE: Many times.
911: OK. The police should be on the way. It just seems like a long time because it's kind of busy in that division right now.

[The yelling in the background continues.]

911, to police: Regarding Gretna Green Way, the suspect is still there and yelling very loudly.
Police Officer on radio: 51 on Gretna Green.
911: Is he still arguing?
[*Knock at the door.*]
911: Was someone knocking on your door?
NICOLE: It was him.
911: He's knocking on your door?
NICOLE: There's a locked bedroom and he's wondering why.
911: Oh. So he's knocking on the locked door?
NICOLE: Yeah. You know what, O.J., that window above you is also open. Could you just go, please? Can I get off the phone?
911: You want, you feel safe hanging up?

NICOLE: [*Inaudible.*]
911: You want to wait 'til the police get there?
NICOLE: Yeah.
911: Nicole?
NICOLE: Yeah.
911: Is he still arguing with you?
NICOLE: Um-hum. He's moved a little [*inaudible*].
911: But the kids are still asleep?
NICOLE: Yes. They're like rocks.
911: What part of the house is he in right now?
NICOLE: Downstairs.
911: Downstairs?
NICOLE: Yes.
911: And you're upstairs?
NICOLE: No, I'm downstairs in the kitchen . . . In the kitchen.

[*Yelling continues in the background.*]

911: Can you see the police, Nicole?
NICOLE: No, but I will go out there right now.
911: OK, you want to go out there?
NICOLE: Yeah.
911: OK, hang up. OK.

Thirteen

For love is strong as death, jealousy cruel as hell.

It blazes like blazing fire, fiercer than any flame.

—Song of Solomon 8:6

CONCLUSION

So, the question remains: How could it happen?

How could a beloved man descend from the pinnacle of professional, athletic and financial success to a seven-by-nine-foot cinder-block jail cell?

How could this Hall-of-Fame athlete, whose photos graced the covers of *Sports Illustrated*, now find his mug shot plastered on the front page of every newspaper in the country?

From the beginning, Orenthal James Simpson had beat the difficult odds stacked against him. An African-American child, afflicted with physically deforming rickets, he'd been brought up by a single mother in a low income section of San Francisco.

The odds were, he wouldn't even make it out of poor Potrero Hill, let alone become a millionaire, an actor, a sports superstar/legend, and a well-respected network sports broadcaster.

But he'd done it.

O.J. Simpson was the kind of self-made man that Americans look up to, and try so hard to emulate.

He was a hero to us, not only because he achieved so much in his life—breaking long-standing athletic records, setting up a profitable company, intelligently managing a successful career—but because he seemed so humble about it all.

He seemed to us a regular guy—not unlike one of his millions of fans who'd cheered him on, first on the 1970s playing fields, "Juice! Juice! Juice!" And then tragically, softly, as a kind of stunned prayer years later when he raced through the Los Angeles streets with a gun to his head.

Though his detractors claim O.J. was slick and profited from his "humble" image, the facts are he was always sharing recognition with his teammates, whom he credited for his successes. And more recently, his friends and professional colleagues sing nothing but his praises.

As his colleagues have testified, over and over again, O.J. was there for them not only on the job but in a personal way.

He exhibited the same drive and I'll-come-through-for-you professionalism in his business dealings as he had as a top athlete.

Yet, these same colleagues, these same teammates and friends, have all had the same reaction to the shocking evidence of what can only be described as another side of O.J.—a side that suggests, at the very least, a dangerous mental instability.

Most everyone was familiar with the much-publicized incident of 1989, in which O.J. was arrested for physically abusing his then wife, Nicole. Friends and colleagues agreed that they believed it was an "isolated" incident.

Yet no one who played with him or worked with him, no one who knew the "professional" O.J. has admitted they knew the real extent of the eight other occasions that Nicole reported physical abuse.

Setting aside the pending murder charges, the abuse was something that has been documented.

Though some may have sensed or suspected something wrong during his years with Nicole and after their divorce, no one could have imagined the extent of the abuse, stalking and harassment that was later revealed.

Many friends and colleagues have since expressed regret that they could have "done something" about it. Could they have helped Nicole and O.J. somehow? Is their story really so different from the many stories of domestic violence across our country?

The question remains at this printing as to the guilt of O.J. Simpson in the murders.

Was O.J. a victim himself, of circumstantial evidence and quickly formed public opinion, based on that evidence? Did O.J. flee from arrest because he was guilty, or because he was truly innocent, distraught and emotional—a man who saw no other way out of a nightmarish situation than to flee?

And if he was guilty, were the murders a crime of passion?

O.J. loved Nicole, he stated it firmly . . .

He said so in a letter he'd written before fleeing the police.

Yet love does not preclude jealousy. And jealousy has produced violence throughout our human existence. Crimes of passion are all too common in our human history.

In her 1992 book *Romantic Jealousy, Understanding and Conquering the Shadow of Love*, Ayala M. Pines, Ph.D. states: "Studies of spousal murder followed by suicide list jealousy as one of the precipitating causes. FBI statistics indicate that about a third of all solved murders involve spouses, lovers, or rivals of the murderer and real or suspected infidelity as a major cause."

In putting forward case studies of romantic jealousy and crimes of passion that follow, she relates: "A study of jealousy-related homicides has identified overt disdain or rejection expressed toward the jealous spouse as an important precipitant of the violent outburst."

The critical role played by a humiliating rejection has been found to be one key trigger to a crime of jealous rage. But was that what really happened on the night of the murders?

That is the vital question that remains unanswered at this printing, as O.J. Simpson sits in his jail cell awaiting arraignment, without bail—on a twenty-four hour suicide watch. The other vital question: *If* O.J. was involved with the murders, did he have an accomplice?

It is the stuff of great drama, great opera—which is one explanation for our rapt attention to such stories.

It is a story that cuts to the quick of our most powerful, and at times most uncontrollable passions.

Watching such stories unfold, we somehow

hope we will find an explanation for behavior, get a handle on how human beings can so easily burst through the fragile boundaries that we try so hard, through the constructs of a civilized society, to keep in place.

In Shakespeare's *Othello*, the nobleman Othello is the archetype of the jealous husband. His firm love for his wife is gradually warped into a jealous rage as he begins to suspect and then believe his beloved wife of infidelity. In a fit of anger, he strangles her. Then, after discovering his suspicions were groundless, he kills himself.

Opera. Drama. Theatre.

All are based on the strange aspects of our human existence.

To see someone we *thought* was a great guy, a guy with a head on his shoulders, a guy with so much going for him, be arrested as the chief suspect in a heinous double murder—to see this shakes us to our core. We want to know the whys and hows.

And so we watch live broadcasts, and read the newspapers, and pick up a quickly put-together biography like this one.

Will we get answers? Perhaps we will, if we look inside ourselves and realize that maybe we are, all of us, just as capable of glorious accomplishments as we are of darker sins.

We cannot forget that in the end, O.J. Simpson's story, and the tragedy of his brutally murdered ex-wife, and her friend, Ronald Lyle Goldman is not drama, or theatre, or opera. Neither is the truth of two children left without a mother.

It is someone's real life.

No matter the outcome of O.J. Simpson's trial, the events that have transpired during one week in the spring of 1994 present a sad and shocking story that cuts to the heart of our humanity, and its many paradoxical and unknowable facets.

The truth is, at the printing of this book, the story of O.J. Simpson is far from finished with the telling.

Yet with his recent arrest, and the revelations that followed, the story of O.J. Simpson remains as one of both:

An American hero, and an American tragedy.

WHO'S WHO IN THE O.J. TRAGEDY

O.J. SIMPSON. He stands accused of "murder with special circumstances." The victims: his ex-wife and a friend. Since the killings, he has been dropped as Hertz Corp.'s spokesman, but he remains on the board of directors at several companies, including Infinity Broadcasting, the nation's largest radio station company, and the Forschner Group which markets Swiss Army knives and Victronix cutlery.

O.J. remains under suicide watch in solitary confinement in a special wing of the Los Angeles County Jail usually reserved for celebrities, former police officers and informers. Outside the Los Angeles Criminal Court, where O.J. was arraigned, a man was peddling a bumper sticker urging, "Pray for O.J."

His career has taken him from the San Francisco projects to a $2 million estate in posh Brentwood, California, but he can currently be reached at :

> Booking Number 4013970
> P.O. Box 86164
> Los Angeles, CA 90086-0164

NICOLE BROWN SIMPSON, Murder Victim. Killed with a friend in front of her luxury Brentwood, California, condominium.

Born in Frankfurt, Germany, raised in Garden Grove, California, a former homecoming queen of Dana Hills high school, she was eighteen years old when she met the then-married O.J. They had lived together for seven years and married in 1985.

They had two children together, but in 1989 O.J. pleaded "no contest" to beating Nicole during a New Year's Eve party. They divorced in 1992.

In recent years, she liked driving her $90,000 white Ferrari Mondiale with the top down, its vanity license plates reading L84AD8—late for a date.

After the tragedy, a former neighbor who lived next door to the Simpsons before their 1992 divorce recalled her impression then: "Sometimes I'd look at the two of them up on their deck and I'd say to myself, 'Wow, what a lucky couple.' "

But Cyndy Garvey, former wife of former baseball star Steve Garvey, has said that Nicole Simpson discussed spousal abuse with her last December. According to Garvey, Nicole said "All they see is the glamor . . . the charming and handsome man next to you, and they don't see your life."

RONALD LYLE GOLDMAN, Victim. At 25, a handsome aspiring model and waiter at the fashionable Brentwood restaurant Mezzaluna.

Police believe he put up a fierce struggle against his killer.

Chicago-born, Ron Goldman had moved to California in 1987. Handsome, 6' 1", he has been described by friends as innocent and naive. He worked out regularly at "The Gym," the luxurious health club where Nicole also trained, and was often seen playing with her children.

He was fond of children, volunteering in hospitals for United Cerebral Palsy and teaching disadvantaged children how to play tennis. "He played an enormous amount of tennis," his father said at a press conference. "He lived for tennis, and at one time he wanted to be a tennis pro."

"It would surprise me not at all if he put up quite a fight, maybe to help Nicole," his father continued. "It does not surprise me that Ron was the prson that offered to return Nicole's glasses. His manager told me he told Ron that he didn't have to, but Ron said, 'I don't mind, she lives close by. I'll be glad to do it.'"

"KATO" KAELIN. O.J. Simpson's young, blond male housekeeper, who appeared before the grand jury on Tuesday, June 22, and, some believe, seriously damaged O.J.'s claim that he was at home at the time of the murders.

A.C. "AL" COWLINGS: The first friend mentioned in O.J.'s apparent suicide note. He grew up with O.J. in Potrero Hill, they played football together at Galileo High in San Francisco, and were fellow members of a social club called the Superiors there.

He drove the white Bronco that led police on a slow-pursuit chase the night of June 17.

"If O.J. could depend on one guy, it was A.C.," former Los Angeles Rams general manager Don Klosterman told the *Los Angeles Times*. There was total loyalty. I'm sure A.C. [didn't] even think he [was] breaking the law, knowing him. He just made a deal to help out his friend."

Their friendship continued at San Francisco City College and the University of Southern Califonia.

"Al followed O.J. like his shadow, both in their youth and afterward," a former teammate told the *Los Angeles Times*. They played together in Buffalo, too, until Cowlings was traded to Houston, then moved on to the Los Angeles Rams. They finished out their careers together with the 49ers.

Cowlings was the gatekeeper at Nicole Simpson's funeral.

ROBERT KARDASHIAN. Longtime friend of O.J., read the letter O.J. Simpson wrote defending himself and thanking friends.

ROBERT K. SHAPIRO, attorney for the defense. Believes that O.J.'s dramatic flight from police who were about to arrest him on Friday, June 17, was part of a suicide attempt, not a desperate escape ploy. "The evidence that I am aware of is that O.J. had no intention whatsoever of leaving the city, the state or the country," said Shapiro. "He was going to the graveside of his wife with the intention of being with her, and, thank God, Al Cowlings talked him out of that and he returned home." A brilliant criminal lawyer, Shapiro is considered a masterful behind-the- scenes legal tactician.

Shapiro was able to convince Erik Menendez to fly home from Israel to face murder charges in the deaths of his parents. He also represented Christian Brando, Vince Coleman, Darryl Strawberry and F. Lee Bailey.

Today he is assembling a team of forensics authorities, including crime reconstruction expert Henry Lee and pathologist Michael

Baden. He frequently tells jurors: "It's better to let 1,000 guilty men go free, than to allow one innocent man to be convicted."

HOWARD WEITZMAN, O.J.'s longtime attorney and personal friend. Two days after guiding O.J. through a three-hour police interrogation about the killings, he withdrew from the case on June 15, citing his personal relationship with O.J. and his heavy workload. "I have decided because of my personal relationship with O.J. Simpson and my many other professional commitments, I can no longer give O.J. the attention he both deserves and needs," he said. "I will continue to advise and consult with O.J. and provide whatever support I can," he said. Weitzman was replaced by Robert K. Shapiro. Ironically, only ten months earlier, Weitzman had succeeded Shapiro as Michael Jackson's chief advocate against a sexual misconduct inquiry.

SUSAN FORWARD, Los Angeles therapist and author of *Obsessive Love: When It Hurts Too Much To Let Go*. After Nicole Simpson's death, Forward revealed that she had counseled her during her divorce from O.J. "O.J. constantly battered her," Forward told a national magazine, "She was terrified of him. He constantly threatened her life. She told me, 'O.J. is so insanely possessive and jealous that there's no telling what he might do. He gets so angry I know he could kill me someday.' "

GIL GARCETTI, Los Angeles County District Attorney. Many LAPD insiders believe he quashed a first-day arrest of O.J. because he wanted a water-tight case, complete with positive forensics tests.

WILLIE WILLIAMS, Los Angeles Police Chief. He has called suggestions that O.J. received special treatment "one of the dumbest statements" he's ever heard.

MARCIA CLARK, lead prosecutor, intends to prove that O.J. acted alone and had intended to commit the June 12 murders. She has not yet decided whether to pursue the death penalty.

PATTI JO MCKAY, Los Angeles Criminal Court Judge, presiding at O.J.'s arraignment, cited the California statute which would allow the state to seek the death penalty or life without parole against him. So far, she has denied Shapiro's request to allow O.J. to have a special cervical pillow to help him sleep in his jail cell.

But she did issue an order allowing O.J. to be examined by his personal doctor.

DR. MICHAEL BADEN, New York State Police Medical Examiner and a forensic pathologist who has been hired by the defense to review all scientific findings and samples.

HENRY LEE, director of the Forensic Science Laboratory in Connecticut and a crime reconstruction expert, has joined the Simpson defense team. He has worked on many celebrated cases including the William Kennedy Smith rape trial, but usually for the prosecution.

PAULA BARBIERI, a beautiful model who has been seen on the cover of *Vogue* magazine and in the *Victoria's Secret* catalogue. She has also been linked to O.J. for years, but she considers him a friend and denies rumors that they were romantically involved. She was mentioned in O.J.'s letter. "Paula, what can I say? You are special," O.J. said in his farewell letter. "I'm sorry I'm not going to have, we're not going to have, our chance. God brought you to me. I now see. As I leave, you'll be in my thoughts.

The letter reportedly shocked Barbieri, her

agent told the *New York Daily News*. "They are like brother and sister," her agent told the press. "Everyone tries to suggest that there is something else going on there, but there just isn't."

THE COMPLETE TEXT OF O.J.'S OPEN LETTER TO HIS FRIENDS

On June 17, O.J. Simpson was scheduled to surrender himself to Los Angeles police to answer murder charges. That morning he suddenly vanished from the house in Encino where he had been in seclusion. While police undertook a vast manhunt, his attorney held a news conference where he was joined by Robert Kardashian. A longtime friend of O.J.'s, Kardashian read aloud the following handwritten letter from O.J. that he left behind when he fled.

First, everyone understand I have nothing to do with Nicole's murder. I loved her. I always have and always will. If we had a problem, it's because I loved her so much.

Recently we came to the understanding that for now we were not right for each other, at least for now. Despite our love we were different and that's why we mutually agreed to go our separate ways. It was tough splitting for a second time, but we both knew it was for the best.

Inside, I had no doubt that in the future we would be close friends or more. Unlike what has been written in the press, Nicole and I had a great relationship most of our lives together. Like all long-term relationships, we had a few ups and downs. I took the heat New Year's 1989 because that's what I was supposed to do. I did not plead no contest for any other reason but to protect our privacy, and was advised it would end the press hype.

I don't want to belabor knocking the press but I can't believe what is being said. Most of it is totally made up. I know you have a job to do but as a last wish, please, please leave my children in peace. Their lives will be tough enough.

I want to send my love and thanks to all my friends. I'm sorry I can't name every one of you. Especially A.C., man thanks for being in my life. The support and friendship I received from so many, Wayne Hughes, Louis Marks, Frank Olsen, Mark Packer, Bender, Bobby Kardashian.

I wish we had spent more time together

in recent years. My golfing buddies, Haas, Alan Austin, Mike, Craig, Bender, Wiler, Sandy, Jay, Donnie, thanks for the fun. All my teammates over the years, Reggie, you were the soul of my pro career; Ahmad, I never stopped being proud of you; Marcus, you got a great lady in Catherine, don't mess it up. Bobby Chandler, thanks for always being there. Skip and Cathy, I love you guys, without you I never would have made it through this far. Marguerite, thanks for the early years. We had some fun. Paula, what can I say? You are special. I'm sorry I'm not going to—we're not going to have our chance. God brought you to me, I now see as I leave you'll be in my thoughts.

I think of my life and feel I've done most of the right things so why do I end up like this? I can't go on. No matter what the outcome people will look and point. I can't take that. I can't subject my children to that. This way they can move on and go on with their lives. Please, if I've done anything worthwhile in my life, let my kids live in peace from you, the press.

I've had a good life. I'm proud of how I lived. My mama taught me to do unto others. I treated people the way I wanted to be treated. I've always tried to be up and helpful. So why is this happening? I'm sorry for the Goldman family. I know how much it hurts.

Nicole and I had a good life together. All this press talk about a rocky relationship was no more than what every long-term relationship experiences. All her friends will confirm that I have been totally loving and understanding of what she's been going through. At times I have felt like a battered husband or boyfriend but I loved her. Make that clear to everyone. And I would take whatever it took to make it work.

Don't feel sorry for me. I've had a great life, great friends. Please think of the real O.J. and not this lost person.

Thanks for making my life special. I hope I helped yours.

Peace and love, O.J.

ABOUT THE AUTHOR

Mark Alan Cerasini is a writer, screen-writer, book editor and editorial consultant. He is the former editor-in-chief of a book review magazine, and he is also the co-author of THE TOM CLANCY COMPANION and a scholarly book on the works of Robert E. Howard. A native of Pittsburgh, Pennsylvania, he now lives in New York City.